Church Organizations Alive!

CHURCH ORGANIZATIONS ALIVE!

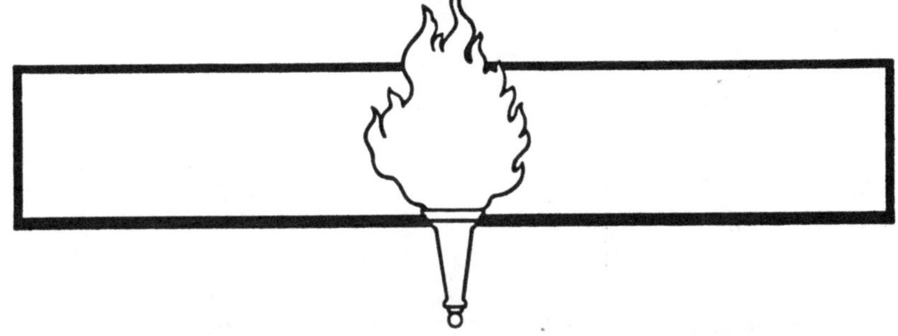

William C. Treadwell
Larry L. McSwain

BROADMAN PRESS
Nashville, Tennessee

4231-15

ISBN: 0-8054-3115-2

Dewey Decimal Classification: 254

Subject Heading: CHURCH ADMINISTRATION

Library of Congress Catalog Number: 86-31745

Printed in the United States of America

Library of Congress Cataloging-in-Publication Data

Treadwell, William C.
Church organizations alive!

(The Broadman leadership series)
1. Church management. I. McSwain, Larry L.
II. Title. III. Series.
BV652.T68 1987 254 86-31745
ISBN 0-8054-3115-2

Dedications

William C. Treadwell, Jr.:

To
Findley Edge

Larry L. McSwain:

To
G. Willis Bennett

Our Mentors in Faith
Our Friends in Ministry
Our Teachers in the Ways of Church

Contents

Preface
1. Organizations Need TLC, Too! 13
2. Birthing Healthy Organizations 27
3. Energizing Volunteer Leaders 41
4. Nurturing Healthy Organizations 60
5. Organization Cry, Too! 75
6. Reinventing the Church 93
7. Let's Celebrate 106
Appendix 1: Models of Church Structures 113
Appendix 2: A Practical Guide to Parliamentary Procedure
by Lee H. McCoy 122
Notes 124
Bibliography 127

Preface

"I hate Wednesdays." The words came from a church business administrator who has the responsibility of organizing a fellowship dinner every week for 450 people in a large metropolitan church.

The same kind of report comes from the chairman of the missions committee. He hates Wednesdays because the committee has met already four times and cannot make a decision about beginning a clothes closet.

The religious educator feels the same way because four groups meet at the same time, and she is supposed to attend them all.

During the 1960s, the eleven-o'clock worship hour on Sunday was called the most irrelevant hour of the week. The ten-o'clock Sunday School hour was called the most wasted. Some would call the 7:00 PM hour on Wednesday the most boring. That is when the organizations of many churches try to do most of their work.

Our purpose in writing this book is to challenge the negative stereotype of the organizational time—Wednesday night. Church is a place of nurture, energy, fun, pain, work, and commitment. Anything that engenders such a range of involvements is neither irrelevant nor wasted.

We want Wednesday evening to be challenging (or any other time the organizations in your church do their work). So we have written this book to help you give leadership to the organizational life of your local congregation. Organizations come alive if the people who lead them give them life.

Sometimes the best way to communicate ideas is through analogies. We have chosen one for the framework of this book. For us, developing church is like raising a child. The process begins with birth and then requires nurturing care and growth toward maturity. There are conflicts along the way which need attention. Still, the conclusion for a mature church organization, as with a grown child, is a celebration. Come with us on the way to enlivening the organizations of your church.

You cannot journey through this book unless you understand something about who we are. We are as different as any two people could be. Yet, eight years ago, we began a partnership that has enriched both of our lives. The team that has coauthored this book and worked in conflict ministry through the years models what we believe about the church of Jesus Christ. One of the great strengths of the church of the risen Lord is its appeal to and acceptance of human diversity. The church needs rich and poor, educated and uneducated, lawyer, plumber, farmer, male and female. All of us stand at the foot of the cross.

Our relationship is one of extreme diversity. In temperament, attitude, background, and skill—in other words, gifts—we differ. Bill is an ex-

football player from Tennessee who loves to play as much as any person alive. Larry is a farm boy from Oklahoma who still works as though today is the last day to get in the crop. Bill is a Christian educator with thirty-three years of practical experience in local churches trying to make the gospel happen. Larry is a seminary teacher whose ideas are as likely to come from books as experience. What we have discovered is that we are one in call, purpose, and commitment. Because of that common core of ministry identity, when we get together our diversity flows into a common strength which generates a bonding stronger than our individual selves. We understand what Jesus meant when he said, "Where two or three are gathered together in my name . . ."

Our approach to church is based on the belief that in diversity the Christian community finds its strength. It is our hope you will find the same strength in the diversity and commitment in your church.

Three words summarize this book. They are: *analysis, theory,* and *common sense.* We have tried to blend them in a way that will be useful in developing commitment to the tasks of ministry through vital organizations. To understand these three concepts, you need to hear a story you will see again in chapter 4.

Bill loves to think about mottoes and folklore. One of the mottoes he used to help his children learn responsible problem solving was: "*Look at it! . . . Think about it! . . . Work it out!*"

> From early childhood, our son Chuck had heard the motto. If something was broken or not assembled, he was taught to look at it, think about it, and work it out! One day we were fishing from the boat and Chuck had a backlash in his casting reel. Passing the rod and reel back to me he said, "Here, Dad, fix this for me, OK?" I chuckled and passed the rod back to him asking, "Chuck, what do we do before we ask for help?"
>
> The memory I recall is of this eight-year-old boy holding the rod and reel with his knees, jerking on the backlash, and muttering, "Look at it" . . . (jerk on the line) . . . "Think about it" . . . (jerk) . . . "Work it out" . . . (jerk).

This story illustrates the approach of the book. "Look at it" is analysis.

So we want you to look at how your church works and understand its functioning. Second, you need some theory about the interactions of organizations in the larger church organism. This is "thinking about it." Finally, "work it out" requires ordinary common sense. We hope you find all three in these pages.

We owe a sincere thank you to Mrs. Penny Long Marler who assisted us in the editing of the final copy of the manuscript.

Let's begin.

1
Organizations Need TLC, Too!

"Tonight is Church Council meeting," moaned pastor Robert Embry at breakfast one hot, summer Tuesday morning. "Another meeting we will have that will probably be a waste of time. I would really enjoy being at this church if it were not for the endless hours of meetings we have. Half the people never attend anyway. And when they do, we sit around and talk about the weather and make no decisions that matter at all."

"Why don't you do away with it?" asked his wife Charlotte, peering over the front page of the morning newspaper, knowing that he neither could nor would do so. "I would if I knew how without looking like a dictator. Half of the decisions we make, I could make in one fourth the time. And better too!"

Seven houses down the street, Thurman Wilkerson was reviewing his daily schedule with his wife Viola. "Let's go to the cafeteria for dinner tonight," he suggested. "I have Church Council meeting to chair at 7:30, and there is no need for us to rush dinner after work. I know you won't get home before 6:00."

"That is the third meeting you have attended at church in the last seven days, T!" (*T* is Thurman's nickname. At least that is what Viola calls him because she has never liked the name Thurman. It reminds her too much of his overbearing father, after whom he had been named.) "What in the world do you ever accomplish at Church Council anyway? All the church business meeting ever gets from the Council is a report of the organizations. Why must our church have so many meetings?"

And so go thousands of conversations on the first Tuesday of every month, or whatever day Church Councils meet, about the frustration of attending church meetings that never seem to matter.

Robert Embry thought about his wife's question as he drove to the church office that morning. Several other concerns flooded his mind at the same time. The day was too crowded. There was mail to be opened this morning. There were calls to make about the stewardship banquet next week. Three hospital visits had to be made, and sermon preparation had to be included somewhere in the schedule. Finally, there was a dull Council meeting to attend.

The Robert Embrys and Thurman Wilkinsons are legion in the church world. Deeply committed to their church and anxious to invest time and energy in its missions, they often feel too much of the organizational life is routine and without life. Robert is like thousands of other pastors serving congregations as the only full-time employee, working with limited secretarial help, and being called upon to do everything imaginable from sitting with the dying to repairing the leaking commode in the women's rest room. Thurman, too, is a carbon copy of the laypersons who love their church, respond willingly to work at the maintenance needs essential to keep it functioning, but want guidance in how to do it with more vigor and success.

We are writing this book for Robert, Thurman, their wives, and the hundreds of men and women who care deeply about the organizational life of the church. Since the book is a partnership, we will communicate to you as one author in most instances. "We" are the narrators of this conversation with you. For we are two ministers who care about helping you work more effectively in giving leadership to the structures of your congregation. Our stories are real, and our suggestions grow out of our experiences. When we describe particular events, we will refer to ourselves individually by name. Otherwise, "we" will communicate with you as one person.

This is a practical book. We want you to enjoy reading it. Join us in trying to understand how we can make the tasks of organizing and leading a congregation interesting, useful, purposeful, and enriching.

Where Is the Ministry in Organizations?

"Organization—2: something organized: a: an organic being or system; organism. b: a group of people that has a more or less constant membership, a body of officers, a purpose, and usually a set of regulations."[1]

"Organism—an entity having an existence independent of or more fundamental than its elements and having distinct members or parts whose relations and powers or properties are determined by their function in the whole."[2]

This is the technical dictionary definition of the subject of this book. More simply, our concerns are how to lead a church so the parts function as a part of the whole. For a good picture of how an organization is supposed to work, one might compare it to the human body. The body is an organism and an organization. For the body to work, the parts must function to support the whole. The church, as an organism and organization works like the body. So the apostle Paul used the body as his model of a ministering church organization.

> Christ is like a single body, which has many parts; it is still one body, even though it is made up of different parts. In the same way, all of us, . . . have been baptized into the one body by the same Spirit, . . .
>
> For the body itself is not made up of only one part, but of many parts. If the foot were to say, "Because I am not a hand, I don't belong to the body," that would not keep it from being a part of the body. And if the ear were to say, "Because I am not an eye, I don't belong to the body," that would not keep it from being a part of the body. If the whole body were just an eye, how could it hear? And if it were only an ear, how could it smell? As it is, however, God put every different part in the body just as he wanted it to be. There would not be a body if it were all only one part! As it is, there are many parts but only one body.
>
> . . . And so there is no division in the body, but all its different parts have the same concern for one another. If one part of the body suffers, all the other parts suffer with it; if one part is praised, all the other parts share its happiness (1 Cor. 12:12-26).

The church is an organism. So is the Church. The New Testamen talks about two kinds of church. One is the Church in its larger sense—the whole collection of believers committed to the lordship of Jesus Christ. This is the Church universal. There is a oneness in the Church that is based upon the common experience of the Holy Spirit by all who confess Jesus Christ as Lord and Savior. The parts of the Church (like the eye and ear Paul described) are the many collections of the church in its local form. This is the second meaning of the church as an organism. The church is also a collection of particular people who gather together to try to fulfill the New Testament understanding of what it means to be the church. We hope you have noticed that we use *Church* to describe this universal organism and *church* to describe the collection of people who make up a congregation of folks who meet at the corner of Second and Main in the neighborhood.

Both understandings of the body of Christ have an organic character. Each is a whole, a body, whose wholeness is greater than the sum of its parts (eyes, ears, and feet). The wholeness of the organism is created in two basic ways. First, there is a wholeness which belongs to the body, yet is created from beyond it. This is theological wholeness. Theological wholeness is that unity which is given to the community of faith by God. Paul said, "God himself has put the body together" (1 Cor. 12:24). Churches do not become whole apart from the work of God in their midst. Thus, the organization of any church has a mysterious, indefinable quality that is based upon this spiritual reality.

Second, as each part of an organism participates consistantly with its God-given gift, another aspect of wholeness is evident. The ear must do its part, namely, act like an ear, if the body is to hear. Likewise, the eyes, feet, hands, and other organs in the body must fulfill their functions. An organism finds its wholeness in the functioning of the organs. This second aspect of organization we call the anthropological side of the church. It is what can be done humanly speaking. It is the aspect of organizations over which the members have control.

The New Testament affirms both sides of this theological-anthropological coin. The Church/church is both human and divine. Theologians call this the *incarnational* character of the church. What that means is that God uses humans in real-life situations to accomplish the plan which

He has had from the creation of the world. That is what Paul described in 2 Corinthians 4:7, "Yet we who have this spiritual treasure are like common clay pots, in order to show that the supreme power belongs to God, not to us."

The ministry in church organization development is birthing and nurturing them so they can fulfill God-given purposes. The physical body needs attention if it is to be healthy. So does the body of Christ.

We will focus in this book upon the practical aspects of designing, developing, altering, and sometimes eliminating structures in the church for purposes of organizational health. Thus, we will focus on the human side of the divine-human reality of the church. This is a structural emphasis, an organizational manual; it is not a theological treatise.

For many persons, attention to organizational matters seems to be a waste of time. It is less than real ministry as a servant response to the needs of persons. It is mundane, time-consuming, nonessential. We feel differently. Organizational service can become all of these things. But whenever this happens, it is because of ineffective organizational service. The reality is that effective ministry has to be organized if it is to be accomplished. Administration is not participation in dull routines of paperwork. The Latin root *administrare* means "to minister to." Administration is the art and science of organizing to serve human need effectively. Dobbins said, "Everything that the minister does of consequence is associated with the administrative function."[3] When the apostles of the early church found the essential tasks of caring for hungry widows was resulting in an imbalance in the total ministry of the church, they organized a special group to give attention to that need (Acts 6:1-7).

We do believe much of the organizational life of today's churches is dull and unnecessary. Many churches lack life because they have fallen into the trap of routine and purposeless meetings. Others are full of conflict because they have not given attention to healthier ways of doing their work. Still others are full of exciting visions which never get accomplished because no structural shape is given to the visions.

Through this book, we hope to help you and your church. It is our purpose to focus upon processes of organizational life which make for effective ministry. The outcome of all meaningful organization is doing a better job fulfilling the intention of God for his churches. It is our dream that this book can be a useful tool for evaluating and reshaping the organizational life of your church so that it becomes an organism full of zest and direction.

Several years ago, Bill was leading a church through a difficult period of conflict. The leaders of the church gathered in a comfortable parlor and began their discussions with negative and harsh comments. Sensing the meeting was going nowhere, Bill threw a pillow to one of the most critical members and asked him to show how he felt toward the church. He then asked him to pass it to the next group member.

Some cuddled the pillow tenderly while others shook it, demonstrating their anger. Finally, when the pillow came to another of the more negative group members, he began to squeeze and hit the pillow to show how frustrated he was with the church. As he did this, a young girl in the group got up from her place and walked to him. Without saying a word, she took the pillow and began to cuddle and weep over it. She was trying to say she loved this church and wanted people to quit abusing it. That was the breakthrough which allowed this group to begin treating the church as an organism to be loved and nourished.

What this group discovered is what every church must discover. Organizations need TLC, too!. Just as every individual needs the affirmation of Tender Loving Care, so do groups, structures, programs, and organizations. How do we express love for an organization?

Intention: Organize with a Clear Sense of Purpose

Organizational care begins with the formation of a structure. Every committee, task force, program, ministry, or organization in a church ought to have a clear purpose. Too often, a structure comes into being in the church because another church formed one, the denomination promoted it, or the pastor asked for it. Sometimes there is no willingness to do away with a task group because of the tradition that has grown up around having it. The first rule of organizational life is: *If you don't need it, don't start it.* The second rule is: *If you don't need it, don't continue it.*

But what is the purpose of any church organization? The answer is simple: *ministry.* No organization is an end in and of itself. It is a means to service. No service, no organization. It's that simple. To decide what ministries for which a church should organize, the New Testament view of ministry is needed.

New Testament Functions of the Church

Many dimensions of ministry are to be found in the New Testament church, so a variety of organizations is needed to fulfill all of the intentions of a biblical church. The New Testament identifies four essential functions or tasks which are to be performed in the church.[4]

Worshiping. The first function of the church is worship. The Westminster Confession has summarized a true biblical insight with its statement, "The highest end of humanity is to glorify God and enjoy Him forever." This may be the clearest definition of worship in Christian history.

Several New Testament words are used for worship. The most common are *doxa* and *leitourgia.* The first refers to the act of glorifying and the second to an act of serving another. Worship is bringing glory to God (doxology) and participating in those deeds which honor God (liturgy). Thus, the highest act of worship in the New Testament is the sacrifice of Jesus Christ (Heb. 8:6; 9:24-28). Worship is accomplished through prayers, giving gifts, singing praises, proclaiming the glory of God, bringing together the people of God in common purpose, and giving oneself as a living sacrifice. Preaching is one of the most important tasks of a worshiping community.

Teaching. The second function of the church is teaching. While worship is the upward look, the educational process is downward deepening in the faith. Among the most important of Jesus' ministries was His creative teaching about the nature of the Law and how one relates to God. His commission to His disciples was to teach all that He had taught them (Matt. 28:19). This function was so important to the early Christians that they developed a manual for the Christian life called the *Didache* which contained instructions for Christians.

Sharing. The third function of the New Testament church is sharing or fellowship. In the New Testament the believers practiced *koinonia* or sharing. The word is often translated "partnership." It refers to the mutual support necessary for true community in the church.

Going. The fourth function of the church is *going.* The noun form of the New Testament root word is *apostolos* from which we get the English word *apostle.* The church is a messenger who is sent to the world to fulfill God's intentions for His people. In going, the church is called as the people of God to share the good news of Jesus Christ in word and in deed to the multitudes outside the church. Sharing verbally is the task of evangelism—telling the good news. This is the commission of the resurrected Lord to His disciples in Matthew 28:19-20. Sharing by means of deeds is the task of service. This is the commission of the earthly Jesus to His disciples in Matthew 25:31-46. Service or *diaconia* is the doing of the good news. Whenever the church fulfills both the doing and telling of the gospel, it is an apostolic congregation, a missionary church. It fulfills the task of being sent by the Father.

Contemporary Functions of the Church

We like to picture these tasks or functions on an axis representing the two dimensions of the church. One, the vertical dimension, is the worshiping-teaching axis. Worship lifts people toward God and away from ourselves. Education deepens people by grounding understanding of the Christian life in the truth of the Scriptures and the knowledge of Christian history. The horizontal dimension is the sharing-going axis. We grow close to each other in the church by sharing the intimacy of our relationship to Christ with each other. This is the journey inward which has as its aim the journey outward in missionary action. The church that is effective in evangelism and service must first be effective in worship, education, and fellowship. The outward reach is the by-product of the inward search.

But to accomplish each of these tasks, a church must have organization. Still, organization by itself is not adequate to fulfill the functions of the church. But how many churches have failed to reach their potential in these four areas because they lacked the leadership to accomplish a worthy objective? This organizing side of the church is recognized in the New Testament as well. It is called the *shepherding* function. The

Greek word is *episkopeo* meaning "to bishop." The bishop is an overseer who is charged with the responsibility of leading the sheep. The shepherd guides and watches out for the sheep. In 1 Peter 2:25, Christ Himself is identified as the "Shepherd and Bishop of your souls" (KJV). Dobbins referred to this function as the "total task" of the minister.[5]

Shepherding is a support function needed for the completion of essential functions we have described. In the contemporary church, this is where buildings, staff, programs, and budgets fit. Seemingly, these four support functions are the reason for existence in some churches. They have become ends in and of themselves. But they are supposed to be the support mechanisms for the primary functions of worship, education, fellowship, and mission. If they do not facilitate these functions, they need redesigning or eliminating. That is what we mean when we say, "Organization follows intention."

Cooperation: Working Together Gets the Job Done

If purpose is the beginning point of all organizational life, cooperation is the primary glue which holds it together. Cooperation is the bonding ingredient that gives wholeness to an organism. Without it, organisms cannot exist.

Covenant

No church can function effectively unless there is a common core of belief which binds its members to each other. Just as the hand cannot live unto itself, so no individual or group within a church can live independently. In Scripture, this common commitment is called a covenant. It is an agreement between God and His people. The foundation of the covenant faith for the church began with Abraham, the father of the Hebrew people. In Genesis 12:1-3, God offered to bless Abraham if he followed His direction. So Abraham left home and began a trek across the desert in search of the promise of God. God kept His end of the bargain by blessing Abraham with a son in his old age. This son, Isaac, became the fulfillment of the promise his father had sought.

Organizations are based on covenants. When a gathering of persons

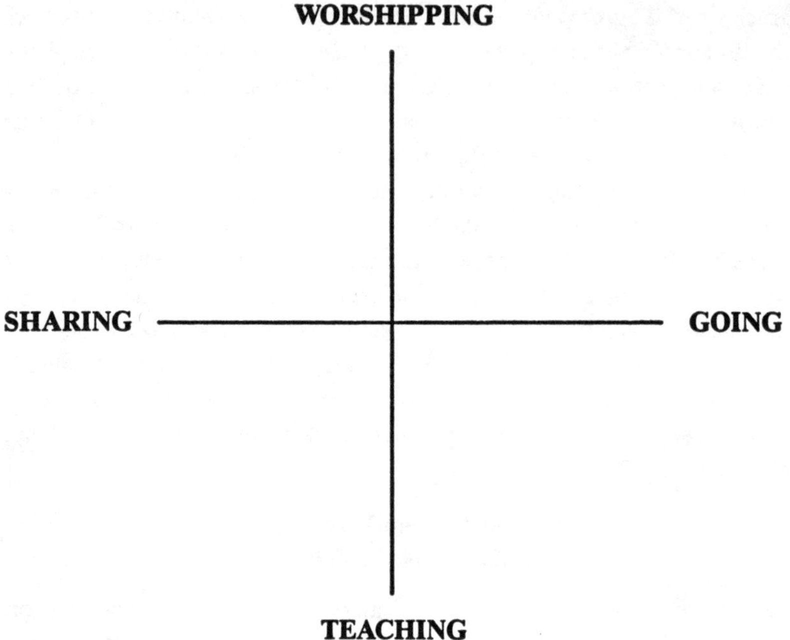

SHEPHERDING

Buildings
Programs
Budgets
Staff

Contemporary Functions of the Church

come together to accomplish a ministry objective, they must have some working agreements if the group is to succeed. Why are we forming this structure? Agreement is needed. To whom is it accountable? Agreement is needed. Who shall serve on it and how shall they be selected? Another need for agreement. What is its relationship to other groups in the church? Get a covenant. How shall we know when its work is finished? Agreement is called for. Cooperation is dependent upon how you start a new structure.

Polity

A shared understanding of authority must precede cooperation. In most church structures there is a polity tradition. Polity spells out the lines of authority. "Who is in charge?" is the authority question. In some churches, the authority clearly resides in one person—a pope or bishop. Any organization within that structure depends upon the agreement of the authority person to act. The authority figure holds the power and can reward or punish accordingly.

In more democratic structures, the question of authority is often unclear or forgotten. The whole group is the authority in a true democracy. So every committee in a democratic group is responsible to the whole congregation for its actions.

In some church polities, there is a mixture of these two pure types of organizations. A small group of persons (presbytery) may be the authority for the church, though the group functions democratically within itself. This is a mixed authority structure.

Organizations fail to work when the traditions of authority are violated or forgotten. Larry worked recently with a church suffering from severe conflict. For five years the church had been in a struggle between competing factions within it. Most of the fighting revolved around the deacons in the church. So the church had changed its bylaws removing the deacons from any administrative responsibilities except as directed by the pastor. Then the pastor had become ill and could not function. When the deacons began functioning as they once had, a faction within the church objected, accusing them of violating the bylaws of the church. Indeed they were violating the bylaws, although no authority was given by the bylaws to anyone except a nonfunctioning pastor. There was no agreement as to who was in charge, so there could be no cooperation.

Noncompetitive Structures

Cooperation requires structures which do not compete with each other. In an ideal church organization, no two groups are given the same responsibility. Each subgroup in a church can contribute best to the whole church if it has a definable function. An ear cannot do the work of the feet if the body is to work. Yet many churches develop their organizations in such a way that multiple persons or groups have been given the same responsibility.

The classic example is the mission offering. In many congregations, mission offerings are promoted by the women's organization. What then, is the role of the finance committee in relation to the mission offerings? Who is to decide how the money is to be spent? Who takes over the promotion task when it is not done? What if the women's organization has poor leadership? If nothing is done, missions suffer. Yet if the finance committee acts, it may be accused of competing with the women of the church. What is the role of a missions committee in such a structure? Can one have an effective missions committee without including representation from the Women's Missionary Society? Hardly!

Cooperative Attitudes

Cooperation is an attitude which persons must share. Well-designed, complementary structures are important in the church, but cooperation comes only from people. The members of the various task organizations of a church must come to their tasks committed to the welfare of the entire body. Cooperation is a spirit of willingness to listen to others. It requires the willingness to give up chosen options when others do not agree with what you want. Cooperative give-and-take is essential for any organization to function well.

Cooperative Decision Making

Cooperation is a process of decision making. Organizations work best when they:

- emphasize the importance of every participant,
- allow individuals to express their feelings and thoughts,
- search for common agreement beyond the separate opinions of any one person and affirm the will of the group.

It is not possible to participate in any organization and secure what you want in every instance. Abiding by the agreements of the larger group rather than insisting upon one's own way, is necessary for cooperation.

Expectations: Work for Something to Happen

One of the requirements of most high-school freshmen is reading a book called *Great Expectations.* A better name for the attitude of many church leaders toward the organizational life of the church would be *low expectations.* No wonder the results are so often pitiful. We believe the results of the church will parallel the investment of energy in its work. "No pain, no gain," has become the slogan of Olympic and marathon runners. It could also be the slogan of the church at work. Where there is no expectation for meaningful investment of time, money, and energy, there will be few results.

For this reason, a clear understanding of the outcome of any organization within the church should be developed before the organization is formed. Older churches can be renewed by reviewing the intended outcomes of every committee and structure with an evaluation of actual results. Clearly written outcomes expected for participation in any group in the church should be settled before people are asked to commit themselves to work at such tasks.

No group should be more aware of such expectations than the nominating committee or persons enlisting involvement from church members. Too often positions are filled for church responsibilities with a casual, "Don't worry, we just need to get your name on our list. The committee really does not do anything except meet a couple of times a year and report to the church annually." Low expectations. Why should anyone make a significant investment in that?

Expect a measurable outcome within a targeted time frame for ever-group within a congregation. Who should determine such expectations? Those who comprise the group responsible for a stated task. And whenever a group changes, review of the expectations for this group will be needed. Changes in membership often require changes in expectations. This is one of the disadvantages of frequently rotating the membership of church organizations.

Larry teaches a number of Doctor-of-Ministry students how to develop new ministry projects in their churches. The most difficult assignment they have is to state clearly their goals for the ministry they intend. Most write vague dreams such as "Our goal is to transform the family life of the congregation." It is a marvelous dream, but how would one know it had been accomplished? Very often such general dreams lead to low expectations. If the same student projects, "My goal is to enlist twelve couples to participate in a marriage-enrichment seminar for each of the next three years," transformation of the family life in the church will be likely. At least you will know where you stand in relation to your goal. Here is a specific agenda with a defined, measurable outcome.

One of the understandable reasons for low expectations in the church is resistance to measure spiritual work. Somehow, evaluation of ministry has become associated with quantifying what is not measurable. How do you measure love? You cannot, except by the deeds of care shown by specific individuals. But to measure the deeds of care is not to invalidate the love which flows from them.

The church which has few or low expectations will achieve the same—very little.

Conclusions

Churches, like people, need tender loving care. Tenderness for an organism is healthy respect for its need for attention. We pay attention to organizations by beginning them with a functional purpose. The loving dimension of organizational TLC is healthy relationships among the people who work in structures. Cooperative attitudes provide the glue for love in administration. Care is based upon attention given to the birth and development of organizations. The following chapter looks at the practical "how-to" of creating TLC for the organizations of your church.

2
Birthing Healthy Organizations

"Why don't we write denominational headquarters and ask them what kind of committees we need?" asked Cecilia Terrell in the planning group of the Newtown Mission. She and five other adults were meeting in her home to discuss plans for beginning a new church in their subdivision. One of the six was their new pastor, a recent seminary graduate. All six were recent arrivals to this brand-new community on the outskirts of a large metropolitan area. "No, I think we ought to design this church to fit our view of mission. We will have more appeal to people here if we are different from other denominational churches," suggested Donald Chanault. "But we have so much to do," responded the pastor, "I doubt we have the time to be creative right now."

Following a devastating toronado in 1974, representatives of the churches in the Crescent Hill community in Louisville, Kentucky, gathered to begin a cooperative community ministry. Several of the ministers in this large urban neighborhood had discussed such a venture for several years. But the toronado forced them to work together in disaster relief in a new way. From this common experience, they wanted to formalize a new organization. Yet they were uncertain as to how it should be structured. How much money should be required from participating churches? How large should the board of directors be? Should the organization be inclusive, allowing the local Baha'i community to join? Or should only confessing Christians be allowed? How much would it cost to incorporate? What ministries should the organization perform? From these questions the United Cresent Hill Ministry was born, but only after months of creative dialogue and meeting together.

"My fifth recommendation to your congregation is to consolidate the administrative structure of your church into a more manageable unit. You now have three commissions and five committees to staff with thirty-five to forty people. That was fine when your church had five-hundred persons in worship attendance. But with one hundred you need a revised organization." The words were those of a planning consultant addressing the Willow View Church which had engaged her to review their future. "I am so glad to hear you say that," responded Dorothy Morgenthau. "We tried to unify our boards three years ago, and the congregation voted it down. But I don't think they understood how much difficulty we are having staffing the work of this church. We are burned out from attending so many committees."

Each of these situations deals with the same issue. How should church organizations be put together? Every church has to struggle with the design of organization or the need for reorganization.

Health for any organization begins at its birth. Many churches never achieve the goal of effectiveness because of the way they were begun. Rudee Boan studied the patterns of success for Southern Baptist missions begun during the years 1979-1984. What he learned is that missions which become strong, self-supporting churches are those which have a good beginning. If there is a strong core of lay leaders committed to the mission at the outset, the chances of success are very high. Failed missions are those with limited leadership, those which are not aggressive in outreach, and those which began depending upon a sponsor or external group for their success.[1] Likewise, individual programs or ministries fail because they have poor beginnings.

Conception: Why Give Birth to Organization?

Every new ministry in a church begins with a vision. Until someone realizes a need to which a church can respond and dreams of a response, no ministry ever takes place. The beginning point of every healthy organization is an idea, a vision, a drive to accomplish. We call this *conception.* To conceive is to imagine what might become of a thought.

A congregation must begin with a clear dream of its purpose.[2] All healthy organizational life grows out of the character of that dream. When the original dream is lost or diminished, it must either be revived or a new dream imagined. Steven Taylor tells a story from Irish history which illustrates the importance of direction in organization:

> Times were hard, and thousands of persons were unemployed. To counter the high unemployment, the Irish government embarked on an ambitious road-building project.
>
> Many new jobs were created. Workers enthusiastically joined the project. Happy to be engaged in a significant task that would both feed their families and benefit their society, the workers sang as they worked.
>
> But after a while, the workers' motivation took a dramatic downturn. The work slowed, and the singing ceased.
>
> Why? The workers discovered the roads led nowhere.

The building project had been concocted just to provide jobs.[3] Dreams provide the road map for a church headed down roads that lead to ministry.

Every committee, program, or structure begun by a church must have a clear relationship to the primary purpose of the church as a body. Organizations will not be organic unless they are needed for the fulfillment of the wholistic mission of the church.

Organization Models Primary Mission

Kennon Callahan suggests twelve keys to the effective church. The first is a clear understanding of the core mission of the congregation.[4] What is the mission of your church? Every organization should add to the ability of the congregation to fulfill its fundamental purpose.

Recent research in varying kinds of congregations has identified four primary mission styles for churches. The first of these is *citizen.*[5] Some congregations view their purpose to be a positive, contributing citizen in the larger community. Such churches tend to be middle-class organizations of business leaders and concerned citizens for whom the church is another means to better the community. The purpose of organizations in the citizen church is to help people understand their community and become more involved in its common life. Such churches tend to lack demanding doctrinal beliefs and any opposition to the larger world. Church is designed not to offend anyone.

The second core mission researchers note is that of *sanctuary*.[6] This kind of congregation seeks to provide a haven from the pressures of the world. The sanctuary church stresses worship and withdrawal from the everyday world. It focuses all it does on what happens at the church building. Such churches may be highly liturgical or informally Pentecostal. Their mission draws the congregation together in worship and mutual support for the fellowship of the church. Such churches often feel warm and supportive to the members present, but seldom reach out to newcomers.

The third style of church mission is *activist*.[7] This church's primary purpose is direct involvement in the needs of persons and groups outside the church. Activist churches tend to become involved in controversial social activities or invest their energies in social ministries to hurting groups.

The *evangelistic* church is the fourth congregational style.[8] Evangelistic churches tend to be young congregations located in growing communities with strong doctrinal beliefs. The primary goal of such churches is growth. They organize to reach out and communicate their message to the community. They work hard to attract newcomers to their church. In reality, a given congregation may have all four of these styles as a part of its heritage. One will, however, be dominant in explaining the core mission of the church.

How does a church communicate its mission? Public image, the preaching style of the minister, the composition, attitudes, and activities of the membership, and the focus of the church's work are all important ways to relate a sense of mission. Organizations become the means of communicating core mission as well. For instance, the congregation in which the worship committee is the most important committee will likely be a sanctuary church; the social action committee will be dominant in the activist church. In the evangelistic church, all organizations will have a defined evangelistic task and work to make everything they do a part of the total evangelism program of the church. Citizen churches will minimize organizational work to free members for community involvements. Look at which structures in the church get the most attention, have the best leaders, and receive the strongest financial support. You can tell much about how that church conceives its mission. A church which has no missions or evangelism committee likely gives little real attention to these concerns.

Organization Defines Participation

Every task has to be organized to get done. All a structure does is provide the means for accomplishing what needs to be done. When Moses led the children of Israel through the Sinai desert, he organized them into groups and established leaders in each group of the tribes so fair justice could be carried out (Ex. 18). When Jesus fed the multitudes, He gave instructions to His disciples so all could be fed (Luke 9:10-17).

Whenever a church is adequately organized, the members have a means for becoming involved. For example, some churches are deliberately organized so that only longtime members have leadership roles. In such a church, everyone knows the only way to get "in" is to stay forever. A church wanting to increase members' participation must organize itself to achieve such a goal. Most people will not participate in that which they do not control. Organization defines membership, who makes decisions, the expected tasks of roles in the church, requirements for participation, and processes for change. Each of these will tend to attract or exclude certain age, cultural, sex, educational, or occupational groups. Churches which allow small groups to make all of the decisions and expect others to implement them will find low levels of participation. So if you want to enlarge the base of participation in the church, enlarge member involvement in the organization of the church.

Organization Shapes Communication

The arrangement of structures affects the way different segments of an organization are coordinated. Coordination is a process of communication. Such a simple matter as the location of church offices may affect the operation of a structure. If the pastor's office is highly visible and lacks privacy, few will seek out the minister for personal counseling. Yet if isolated from the flow of office work, the minister may miss opportunities to talk informally with staff workers, volunteers, or unexpected visitors. Much informal communication is lost. Every organization has advantages and disadvantages.

Simple and clearly understood structure results in direct and accurate communication. As organizations grow they add layers and become bureaucratic. A bureacracy requires expert management and control. The larger and more complex the organization of the church, the more difficult it will be for the members to understand the work of the congregation. Effective leaders design and birth organizations which provide maximum communication within and between all of the parts of the church body. Exactly how that is done is what we call a "systems" question. Follow as we divert you briefly into a discussion of theory which can help you decide how you need to structure your ministry organization.

Gestation: Planning for Healthy Organizations

Organizing takes time. In the same way it takes months from the time of conception of a child until its birth, churches need time to plan healthy organizations. What are the questions one must answer in moving from that first idea of a need for ministry until the action occurs to bring it into being? Ronald G. Capelle suggests every organization functions as a logical system. It has certain clearly definable elements. Our modification of his model of the elements of an organizational system provides the elements for a systematic process for planning a new organization.[9]

Most church folks do not think in such highly structured ways, so we want to identify the systems questions one answers in birthing an organization.

Output: What Outcome Do You Expect?

John Roberts seldom presents a new idea to the Church Council that

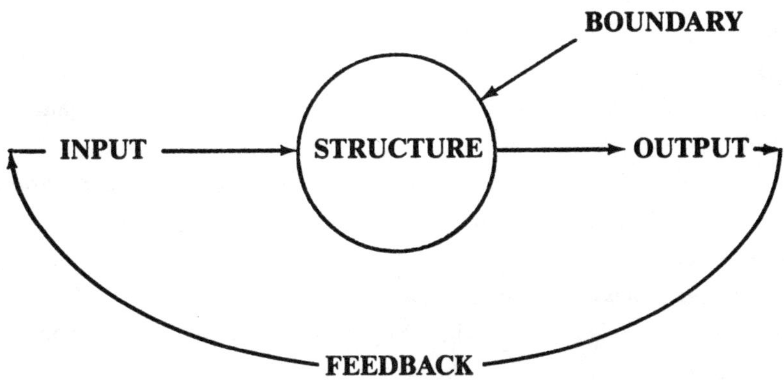

Elements of an Organizational System

is not shot down by Herman Gottwald. John is the pastor of the New Harmony Church where he has served for slightly more than three years. During this time, John has spent four weeks each year studying at a distant seminary to earn a Doctor of Ministry degree. The first Council meeting after he returns each year, John usually proposes a new organization for the church. It seems John is working on a project in organizational management at the school, and his professors are constantly encouraging him to redo the structures of the church.

Herman does not try to be an irritant. But John thinks he is. "Every idea I present to this Council is resisted by you, Herman. I do not understand why?"

"It is quite simple," Herman replies. "You are always wanting to change things for the wrong reason. You propose things without telling us what will happen if we do it. Isn't it one of Murphy's laws that says, 'If it ain't broke, don't fix it'? I want to know what we can expect from another committee. Half those we have now never meet."

Every church has at least one Herman. If there were more, churches would be healthier. His concern is the beginning point of organizing ministry.

What do you want to take place because of this committee, program, or structure? Such a question is easily answered in industry. The outcome or output of a factory is a product. So organization focuses upon the best way to make a widget. But churches are not factories. The hardest task they often have is defining what they want to happen. The outcome of church organizations should be one of the following:

- Persons in the church feel a greater sense of intimacy with each other because of what the organization has done.
- New persons decide to become a part of the church.
- A need felt by a member or person known by the congregation is met.
- Church members decide to participate more faithfully in the worship and work of the church.
- A greater amount of money is given to the church.
- Conflicts within the church are concluded.
- A specific task is accomplished.

If you cannot state the intended outcome of a new structure you are considering, it may not be needed.

Input: What Resources Do We Have to Achieve this Outcome?

Unhealthy organizations often emerge because the church desires results beyond its means. Larry was engaged in a planning consultation with a declining Anglo church in a Hispanic community:

> I was encouraging the church to dream a new dream of a realistic size and ministry potential. The church had declined from 950 in Sunday School to 200 and had a budget of $175,000. Nearly half of the members were over age 65. During the discussion session, a rather eccentric man rose to argue forcefully for beginning a television ministry. "If we would go buy the cameras and get on television like First Church, we could fill this church in two weeks." When I reminded him of the cost of such a venture, he simply argued more loudly for his idea.

The outcome of a television ministry was certainly a challenging dream for that church. But it was being argued by a person with no resources to aid the dream. He lived on Social Security, had been in the church two years, and had no knowledge of the complexities of a television ministry. He knew the outcome he wanted, but this church did not have the resources to make it happen.

The second step of organizational planning is to assess the resources available which can be applied to the expected results. Again, the resources available to a church are unlike those in business and educational organizations. The church leader must understand that all church resources are voluntary. No means is available for coercing from others what is needed for functioning in ministry.

Few church members provide all of the resources they are capable of giving, however. Thus, a major planning task is to find a means of motivating greater commitment from church members to supply available resources for the desired tasks of ministry.

What are the kinds of resources which can be secured for appropriate organizational objectives?

Creative ideas. Every church has members with the special talent of envisioning new ways of exciting, attracting, and involving people in

Christian service. If the intended result or a new ministry requires a new approach, willing, creative minds are an asset.

Time and Energy. Who will do the work required to produce the desired outcome? Churches exist because of the efforts of volunteers. If they are not available, the intended ministry cannot take place. Churches today face problems in this area as many of the volunteers of the past, namely housewives, are now working outside the home. These women have less time available for church work. Increasingly, churches must rely upon retirees. Often these volunteers want to retire from church also.

Money. Because of declining sources for volunteers, churches often think of adding staff to do the work necessary to produce a new outcome. Raising additional money may be the easiest means to provide new sources of time and energy.

Prayer. No new venture should be attempted if there will not be commitment of prayer for it. Identifying the persons who will commit themselves to pray for intended outcomes releases the power of God to lift a group beyond the resources they thought were available to them.

One of the major difficulties of treating a church in systems terms is the unpredictability of available resources. One is not always able to know what resources can be generated for a given outcome. This makes church planning a sometimes frustrating venture.

Structure: How Do You Link Resources to Intented Outcome?

There is a broad range of choices available in designing an overall church structure. Rather than provide the details of how churches can be designed, we have summarized organizational theories in Appendix 1. If you are working on the overall design of your organization, consult the appendix. There you will find descriptions and visual designs for:

- A simple design for small churches.
- A brief discussion of resources for denominational designs.
- An appraisal of strengths and weaknesses of advisory organizations.
- A commission or committee organizational design.
- A strong Church Council organizational design.

- A central power group approach to organization.
- An interchurch organizational model.
- A process approach to dealing with organizational concerns.

When planners are clear about a new organization's purpose (outcome) and have made an assessment of available resources, the two must be brought together in some workable structure. This is the heart of the organizational task. We believe the simpler this is done, the more effectively the organization will work.

Not all churches have a choice about the structures they will develop within their congregation. Generally, churches in the more liturgical and hierarchical traditions have their structures determined for them by books of discipline, directives of bishops, canon law, or some other kind of established expectation. Most churches in the Baptist or congregational tradition have considerable freedom to choose how they wish to organize. Even so, subtle pressures may come from denominational leaders or the need to conform to what other congregations do. In making their choice, church leaders need to be aware of the possibilities for selecting an organizational approach.

We believe there are two pitfalls you must avoid as you lead your congregation. One is the idea that there is an ideal structure for your church. The church is made up of people. Whenever more attention is given to structures than persons, the priorities of the church have been misplaced. Structures should be a way people get together, work together, and grow together. The second pitfall to avoid is the idea that some one else can design your church's organization for you. Others can help. But your congregation must make its own choices about how it will work.

Feedback: How Will You Know You Have Succeeded?

The final step in the planning process for healthy organizational life is evaluation. Too often a church begins a new organization and never asks whether it is accomplishing what it intended. Evaluation is the means for feedback in the organization. It should always be done at stated intervals after the initiation of a new ministry. Evaluation will raise the following questions:

- Was the outcome we intended achieved?
- If not, did we fail to define adequately what we expected?
- If not, did we fail to assess our resources correctly?
- If not, did we fail to develop adequate structure?
- If not, did the persons accountable to do specific tasks fulfill them?
- If not, can we refine our intended outcome?
- If not, can we reassess our resources and achieve part of our intended results?
- If not, can we restructure and do what we intended?
- If not, can we replace irresponsible persons with individuals who will fulfill the tasks of the structure?
- Do we need to terminate this effort? This question must be raised whether the effort succeeded or failed.

How Big Should the Structure Be?

The size of the organization should be determined carefully. How large a structure should be is a matter of the size of the church, the need for representation, the task at hand, and available personnel. A group designed to promote intimacy should have no more than eight members. Policy-making groups need to be large enough to represent fully all elements of the congregation: young, old, male, female, economic-class groups, and ethnic groups. A task group or study group could be quite large.

The size of the group will also affect what kinds of leadership are needed, where the group meets, and how a meeting is organized. Lyle Schaller offers several helpful ideas on the difference between the work of a small group and a large group. Large groups need carefully planned agendas, the focus is on the leader, and the arrangement of the room promotes formality. The opposite is the case in each instance for the small group. Small groups can meet much longer without breaks and require less formal agenda than large ones. Select a size that is functional to the needs of the organization you are birthing.[10]

Delivery: Giving Form to the Plan

Conception and gestation are processes necessary for birth to occur. Once the specific needs for organization are clear, the work of giving shape to the discussions, thought, and plans is done.

Write It Down

1. Put on paper exactly what the organization is designed to do. Write the purpose in specific terms.
2. Indicate the number of persons needed for the organization to function smoothly.
3. Outline the responsibilities of the group. What does it need to do? How frequently does the group need to meet? What are its relationships to other organizations in the church?
4. What will it cost? If budgeted funds are needed, it is best to state these expenses at the beginning. How much time will be required by how many persons to accomplish the purpose?
5. To whom is the group accountable? How are they expected to report, with what frequency, and in what form?

Decide Who Should Approve

Major new ventures will require congregational approval. Any long-term or standing committee should be presented through all of the channels of the church for formal support. In such cases, the matters described above should be added to the bylaws or an organizational manual.

Short-term or one-time organizations may not need congregational approval but would need the concurrence of a board, staff, or pastor. Committees such as finance may need to be consulted. Work with the structure which is a part of the tradition of your congregation.

Communicate Clearly to the Approval Group

Many fine designs have fallen on stoney ground because of a poorly presented plan. Use multiple messages to communicate the need for this new venture. Show pictures of the need. Ask influential persons to share orally why such a beginning should be supported. Put in clear written form what the organization will do, how, and by whom. Remember, any new structure will have to be sold to those who are asked to support it. Finally, have the plan presented by the power leaders of the approval group.

Fit the Organization into the Structure

If the organization is worth all of the work done to develop it, be sure it becomes a part of the formal life of the church. Voted actions duly recorded in the minutes of the approval group will avoid later questions as to what exactly was done. Again, write the action into the bylaws, policies, or manuals of the church.

Nurture: Commitment to Care

The newer an organization, the greater its need for nurturing. Like a newborn infant, a new structure will be highly dependent on those who brought it into being. It takes at least six or more meetings before any new group can be ready to begin functioning with some independence. So, plan to invest considerable energy in the first year of any new effort. The larger the effort, the longer the time frame for creating independence.

Nurturing is the personal dimension involved in any group, regardless of its purpose. The next two chapters guide you in the things you can do to keep the nurturing touch in organizational leadership. The first task is developing the leadership resources needed for vitality. The second is effectively managing to keep the organization on target.

3
Energizing Voluntary Leaders

The process of finding and motivating leaders for the church has often been called the "fuss-and-beg" process. Every person who has ever served on a nominating committee knows how difficult it is to recruit the necessary leadership for fulfilling the goals of the organization. The nominating process usually begins with noble calls for volunteers to work in the life of the church. From the pulpit and within the newletter comes the appeal of the "high road."

> Want an opportunity to serve Christ and His church? The nominating committee has begun its task of securing teachers, workers, and committee members for the coming year. Won't you volunteer to the committee? Tell them the spiritual gift that is yours and the area of ministry where you would like to serve.

By the time the committee is within one month of its report to the church, the message has moved to the level of guilt and duty. Now the pressure from the pulpit and newsletter is:

> Every Christian ought to serve the church in some special way.
>
> If we don't find a teacher for the youth group soon, we will fail them in their need for Bible study.
>
> Do you want your grandchildren to go unattended in the nursery?

Then the committee shifts downward again and goes on a personal campaign to plead and beg for workers. Over the telephone goes the cry, "I am sure you will reap joy from the work." "God will bless you and your efforts if you will only do it." "*Please* help us; there is nobody else to ask."

Finally, the committee demeans the job with statements like, "There is not much to this," or, "The group will meet only once this year and then report," or, "The work is not that time consuming, so if you will let us list your name, I am sure it will be no trouble."

So it is not too surprising after our workers are in place, the scenario they adopt is the same routine. When momentum starts to slip and motivation is low, the support staff or group leader will fuss at the group or beg them to be more responsible. After all, that is how they were enlisted. "If it worked once, maybe it will work again," we say. The results of fussing and begging are usually negative. Conflict, hurt feelings, and sometimes even resignations are a result.

Low morale and resignations trigger a panic in church leadership, and then more begging is employed. "Please stay with us. We need you! We are almost finished with this job and at least see us through the church meeting next month."

This self-defeating system or cycle can be broken if we will:

- Select leaders with commitment.
- Recruit with integrity.
- Support group members with tenacity.
- Reward people with intentionality.
- Change the effects of punishment in church.

Select Leaders with Commitment

Vitality in any organization is the product of energetic leaders. The development of a dynamic church requires enlisting leaders who are enthusiastic and excited about ministry.

Several helpful understandings of Christian leadership have been developed, including other books in this leadership series.[1] While we will not duplicate these efforts, the dimension of leadership in organizations is an essential emphasis. Three fundamental approaches affect leadership style. These are:

1. A relational approach which emphasizes personal interaction in

leadership. The relational leader stresses the feeling level in a group and tends to give priority to maintaining caring and supportive feelings between the members of a group.

2. A process approach focuses attention upon the steps one follows in moving from a need to a response in ministry. The need may be a problem, an issue, a service to be performed, a decision to be made, or a program to be developed. The process leader tends to be more concerned for how a need is met than what is done to meet it.

3. Task-oriented approaches give attention to what needs to be done. Task-oriented leaders do not necessarily ignore feelings or processes, but they are unwilling to allow either to stand in the way of the completion of the task. This approach emphasizes getting the job done.

Robert Dale suggests four leader styles which stress these approaches in differing ways. The *catalytic* leader employs all three approaches in an effective active-positive approach. This leader is aggressive at doing the task but follows good processes with attention to people. The *encourager* stresses the more relational side of leadership. This person is a passive-positive leader who stresses feelings and fellowship.

A third leader style is the *commander*. This active-negative style stresses the tasks to be done. Feelings will be ignored, if necessary, to finish the job. Finally, the *hermit* is an eroding style functioning passively and negatively. The hermit avoids both personal relationships and tasks. It is a highly ineffective style.[2]

Obviously, churches need all kinds of leaders. Some leadership assignments call us to dream, analyze, plan, and conceptualize in our churches. Process leaders work best at these tasks. Other assignments require skilled relational support and smoothing and resolving of differences. But most church assignments require a clear-cut task orientation. Thus, we are focusing upon how you get the job done in this chapter. Finding good leaders is no easy task. But some guidelines will help.

First, look for your church leaders in the pool of community leaders. Good church leaders are usually good community leaders and competition for their time and energy is fierce in a day of intense national and local community volunteerism. If you want healthy church organizations, seek leaders with experience and skill to give overall guidance and primary leadership to church tasks.

Second, we believe leaders should be recruited from the active believer core of the congregation. Churches dare not play games at this point. Do you remember the nominating committee discussion which went: "Mary Reynolds is not very active anymore. Let's give her a job, and maybe she will become more involved?" Or, "Tom Jacobs is straying from the church. He used to be here every time the doors were opened. Let's elect him to the Personnel Committee, and he'll come back." Or, "Sarah Wilkinson's husband is not a member. If we put them both on the Building Committee, possibly he'll get hooked and join the church."

Our conviction is that potential leaders demonstrate their attitudes and loyalties with interest and involvement. Leaders should be chosen from among those who demonstrate concern in the worship, education, and ministry of the church. Potential leaders can be trained, given skills, and information. They can be developed into outstanding relational, process, and task-oriented servants if they have received divine energy and a sense of call to involvement.

Where that calling has not been demonstrated, another focus is needed. For members and friends of our churches who have not expressed this sense of energy and call, we need to engage in discipleship training. It is not leadership training they need, but nurturing in the faith through careful personal development of their Christian commitment.

Third, the leadership core of a congregation must be representative of the church in age, education, church experience, and vision. What we are calling for is balance—a cross section of the total church. Since most church programs are task oriented, each committee or group should have a majority of task-oriented leaders with some process and relational leaders. Our experience in dealing with conflict indicates difficulty arises when any task group in the church lacks representation from the diversity of the larger church or lacks balance in leadership styles.

Beware of the programmatic commander who is not sensitive to people. Look for achievers with patience and integrity, men and women who will be governed in their drive to achieve by love of people.

We assume that you use the tried and proven principles of a search team or nominating committee in your search for good leaders. We would add both the instrument of a *musing board* and a preselection step. The musing board is a flip chart, chalk board, or marker board mounted where you can sit and study it. Write the purpose of an organization or committee on it. Then list the workers now serving. Back your chair away, sit and muse/think about each leader. Who are they? What is their world like? Do they have time and energy for the task? Are the people who make up this leadership team alike? Is there a good balance between chiefs and Indians, between thinkers and doers, experience and energy?

When you identify the specific needs of your group, take a church roll or directory and search for those who would bring balance to your group. This preselection will help you communicate to the nominating group committee needs and offer specific suggestions.

Warning! If you are a minister, an educator, a Sunday School director, or any responsible leader who is using the musing board and preselection process, beware of the tendency to place your friends and supporters in leadership. Avoid using your influence to boycott people who do not see the church your way. Proper balance produces better decisions in the church than a stacked deck. The struggles on the leadership teams will be honest and representative of the congregation if this concept is followed faithfully. The tendency of selecting supporters and punishing opponents creates leadership groups which run too far ahead of the larger congregation. Conflict potential is high when this happens.

Our last suggestion about leadership selection has to do with leadership history which we call *acceptable predictability.* If we are to work as teams in our leadership groups, we must know each other and be able to predict reactions and attitudes. Such predictability lowers the anxiety of interaction and facilitates community feelings in the group. Thus, the key to the leadership core's morale is not just that we have a high level of predictability for each other, but that the predictable behavior is acceptable.

In one of the churches Bill has served, a member of an important committee would stand up and walk out when the discussion did not go his way. Members could anticipate what he would do, but they could not accept his action. His behavior destroyed the potential for health in the group. Performance, past personality traits, attendance habits, and time awareness all add to our ability to predict how people might perform as leaders. Choose those whose predictability is acceptable and positive.

Recruit with Integrity

Integrity in the recruitment of volunteer workers requires two principles: honesty in expectations and consistency between those expectations and the abilities and resources of volunteers. Church leaders are often frustrated with the task of securing volunteers for church work because they are staffing a dishonest system. That is rather strong language. What do we mean? Perhaps an illustration will help.

Margaret Williams teaches planning and church leadership in a theological seminary. During her sabbatical, she volunteered to serve on the long-range planning committee of Calvary Church in the new city where she was studying. The committee was very frustrated with their difficulty in adequately staffing the committees and programs of the church. The biggest complaint in the church was that members were overloaded with too many assignments. Margaret decided to study the organizational structure of the church. When she wrote down every task being attempted, the rotation system used, and the size of each group required by church bylaws, she was shocked! A total of seventy adults participated in the church. Yet the committee structure alone required one-hundred people. No wonder *burnout* was the most frequently used word in the congregation. The church had a dishonest system.

Margaret redesigned the task requirements of the church by combining several committees into one, simplifying the structure. Then the size of each committee was reduced. The people responded enthusiastically to a new organization in which they could work vigorously at one or two jobs with clear feelings of success in accomplishing them. They could be honest in making commitments to tasks of interest.

Recruitment with integrity begins in recognizing that not all church members will commit themselves to volunteer service. We believe the 50/50, 70/30, and 80/20 rules work in most congregations. The 50/50 rule states that half the membership of a church will participate regularly and support the work of the church financially. The 70/30 rule states that of this participating and supporting half, 70 percent will not volunteer for formal, continuing work responsibilities at any one time. Thus, the volunteer pool within the church is no larger than 30 percent of the participating, supporting core of the membership. The only way an organization can be expanded is by enlarging the participating, supporting core. The 80/20 rule states that 20 percent of the participating members will do 80 percent of the work and give the leadership to raise 80 percent of the money in the church.[3] Thus, the organizational structure for effective functioning needs to be designed to fit a volunteer size no larger than 30 percent of the active members.

But how do you recruit the 30 percent?

1. Identify potential workers. Church leaders have a tendency to seek involvement from persons who are already involved. This is quite appropriate for the visible leadership roles essential for the church. But many

tasks are required which a wide variety of persons can do. Ignore no one. The overlooked are often a source for workers:

- Shut-in members who can be telephone callers.
- Handicapped persons confined to wheelchairs who can type at home.
- Newcomers who are enthused about the church but not known by others. Training them as ushers gives them the opportunity to meet church members.
- The shy who will never volunteer, but will do excellent work if asked to do a task with which they are comfortable.
- Teenagers. More mature high school students can teach and care for younger children and participate in a host of activities.
- Retired persons who have available time on a seasonal basis, even though they may travel extensively during certain times of the year.
- Young mothers working at home who may not be able to work at the church building but will do a variety of tasks at home.
- Widows who have no transportation but have free time if transportation is available.

2. Depend upon primary workers to identify their friends. In larger churches especially, the key to finding workers is often to enlist a leader to take responsibility for recruiting others needed to fulfill his or her area of responsibility. If this is done, however, be sure there is consultation with the overall leadership of the church to insure that the goals of the organization are understood. Just selecting friends may not result in fulfilling the objectives of a committee or task group.

3. Discover the interests of the people. Too often people are only asked to do those tasks similar to their professional or occupational work without knowing of other interests. A teacher in the public school might prefer to organize a mission project rather than teach in the church. When newcomers join the church, a list of interests and talents should be requested for future reference.

4. Review the church membership to find those on a "leave of absense." Burnout is a reality for church folks as much as anyone else. Sometimes dedicated leaders take a leave of absence after years of con-

BAR-ROOM
BAR-ROOM
BEE BEEP
BEE BEEP
BT/86
IT TAKES ALL OF OUR VOICES TO MAKE MUSIC!

stant volunteer service. They need some refilling of their spiritual selves with new enthusiasm and energy. This is appropriate and should be encouraged. In fact, most churches have some kind of rotation system for committee members and teachers to protect them from becoming bored with their work in the congregation.

But the tendency to take a permanent leave of absence is not healthy. Former workhorses who have decided to rest awhile may become overly comfortable with the rest routine. Encouragement will be needed to reactivate the resting for roles of leadership.

5. Don't forget the folks who grew up in the church. It is not unusual for the church to overlook the longtime member whom everyone knows and who is not recognized for outstanding achievements. This will be especially true if the person works at a blue-collar job. A thoroughly committed carpenter who has been in the church twenty years may be bypassed for deacon while the new doctor in town is chosen immediately.

6. Develop a leadership pool. One church in North Carolina works hard to create a potential leadership pool. The church has a training committee in place that manages a course in Christian discipleship and another in general principles of leadership. Careful attention is given to developing these classes as models for future leaders. Participants include newcomers to the church and workers who need a rest between assignments.

A philosophy of discipleship is studied in the classes. Also a search for spiritual gifts is conducted with the crucial tie made between the gifts of the individual, the call of God to serve, and the specifics of working in small groups of volunteers. This is one serious and valuable way to enrich a church's core of workers.

7. Select leaders who can be supported in fulfilling their jobs. Pastoral, staff, and key lay leaders are responsible for giving attention, encouragement, and assistance to volunteers when they are in trouble. To do so requires a commitment to the volunteer group. Several important questions need clarifying if support is to be given:

• Is this person an active member of the church? Effective service requires a commitment to the organization served. Those on the outside can hardly be enthusiastic about a church until they make a commitment in the forms of membership, attendance, and financial support.

• Is this person one who usually gets along with others? The ministry of the church requires relational skills for most tasks. To choose a person who angers others, creates distance, or discourages others is to invite nonsupport.

• Will this person be open to cooperation with the pastor, staff, and key lay leaders? While one never wants lackeys on the team, harsh critics and resisters to every effort of the key leaders of the church create low morale and sap energy.

• Can this person understand the purpose of the church and the relationship of their specific tasks to that purpose?

• Does this person have enough time and energy to do this task well? Selecting persons overwhelmed with work outside the church simply depresses others in the church when they have to cover for the individual who cannot get the tasks done.

• What specific gift or expertise does this person bring to the group?

• Has this person been too prominent or visible in the life of the church over the past three years? At times overexposure to a good leader results in lack of initiative from others or lack of interest in new leaders. Repetitious use of the same outstanding leaders creates the sense of a power bloc and decreases ability of others to do a good job.

Most churches have not reached the level of sophistication we are describing. You must use who is available and willing. We have emphasized the importance of this organizational work at the risk of repetition in this chapter. Let us remind you to be serious, prayerful, and upfront about tasks and expectations you have for workers if the church is to be exciting.

You ought to see a clear truth emerging in this material. *Those who work in the leadership roles of the church must be enlisted with the utmost care and treated with as much love and respect as those whom we are trying to reach on the outside.* It makes little sense psychologically and none spiritually for us to treat those who work in God's kingdom with less concern than we have for those outside the Kingdom. Therefore, those responsible for task groups in the church must have a double focus:

—Love and concern for the group—
—A deep sense of call to the tasks needed by the church—[4]

Support Group Members with Tenacity

Bill received a long-distance telephone call from a pastor friend with a leadership problem. The strong church the friend served was in a program to finance a new building program. The friend told this story.

> The chairman of deacons is also chairman of the building program in our church. For the past year he has given outstanding leadership, working on location problems for the new building and leading in our fund-raising campaign. The church has $200,000 collected already and pledges for another $350,000 which will complete this building. Last night was our last meeting for final approval to break ground for the building on the first of the month. I went to the meeting expecting absolutely no problems in moving forward. My first surprise came when the chairman resigned in the afternoon deacons' meeting prior to the congregational meeting. Little was said about his decision. Everyone assumed he resigned so he could give more attention to the building. We all looked forward to the business meeting.
>
> The surprise escalated when the chairman of the Building Committee stood and, instead of presenting the motion everyone expected, launched into an attack on the entire project. He said the church neither wanted nor needed the new building, spoke harshly about those who wanted the program, downgraded our motives and sense of judgment. He then resigned as chairman of the building effort.
>
> Our church is angry. I am angry! No, I am so mad I can hardly see! Today people have been calling to cancel their pledges, and others are raising questions about two years of hard work. What can I do?

Bill asked the pastor a simple question. "What is going on in Mr. Alexander's life?" They discussed the question, and the pastor agreed to find out and call back later. Two days later he called back. "How could I have missed what has been going on in this man's life? I checked up on John Alexander and found out about three major events of physical, professional, and family crises in his life in the last three weeks. Now I understand why he acted the way he did."

We believe it is easy to miss a major change in the lives of the church's leadership core. We have to work at knowing how they are doing and what is happening in their worlds. It took that church a whole year to regain what was lost in one night. There is much to learn in this short case study. Let's begin by stating one of our major premises—*Every leader must have good information and a positive relationship with the church's task teams to offer meaningful support if those teams are to function with health.*

But who will maintain this caring personal contact with the core leadership of the congregation? We believe that must be a part of the responsibility of those who provide leadership. The pastor or staff should work to keep up with chairpersons and major division leaders of the church organization. In turn, these leaders can be functional links to each of the persons with whom they work. Thus, the chairperson of a committee or the department leader of the Sunday School is the first line of contact for professional leaders in moving toward the troubled work force of the church. It is a matter of organization. Pastoral caring and healthy organization fit together like the hands of a couple in love.

Reward Group Workers with Intentionality

Energy for the tasks of ministry is also stimulated by reward. Churches often fail to reward their workers with positive affirmation. In some cases, intended reward turns to negative embarrassment.

Bill loves to tell the story of an associational meeting he attended during seminary days. His religious-education professor had given the class an assignment to attend the meeting and to take notes on how the Baptist Association communicated its goals for the year and rewarded its workers. After the song service, across the stage, and under the spotlights, came young ladies in long evening dresses. They carried cards with numbers painted on them. A narrator told the audience, "The young lady in blue is Sally Jones, the pride and joy of Mark Valley Baptist Church, and she is carrying the goal for the new Church Training units in the association this year!" There were twelve girls carrying signs with goals. One girl had her sign upside down, and another nearly dropped hers. The audience roared with laughter, the girls were embarrassed, and the narrator was dumbfounded.

At the same meeting, men and women were asked to come to the stage and be introduced by office. They were also asked to say a few words about their work. Obviously, none of the people were told in advance they were to do this. The spotlight would follow them up the steps and across the stage. Each would stumble through an uncomfortable speech. They showed such discomfort, the audience continued laughing at every stumble and awkward facial expression.

The final attempt at rewarding was no better. People were asked to stand when their names were called for recognition of their involvement in the association. The spotlight would search for them in the audience after they stood. At least one third of the people called out were not present. As the spotlight searched for the absent people, the narrator nervously searched for words. As the laughter in the audience increased, the narrator had to raise his voice. While funny, the evening was a fiasco.

It is one thing to laugh and enjoy Christian fellowship. It is quite another to laugh at Christian workers and their work. It is even worse to be laughed at as a Christian worker by the people you serve.

Lyle Schaller has a helpful discussion on what he calls "silver beavers and dead rats." The "Silver Beaver" is a distinguished service award begun by the Boy Scouts of America in 1931. Silver beavers are what churches give their leaders when they reward them with satisfaction for the work they do. "Dead rats" are negative rewards and/or the simple oversight of many who work diligently.[5]

A good reward procedure focuses on the group and its tasks. Every "thank you" written personally or printed in church publications and every verbal statement of appreciation should include a short review of the work and achievement of the team. Such notes of recognition should state who led the team and give a clear indication of how the effort is related to the overall work of God in that place.

When rewards are designed not merely to feed egos, they reveal team values and church dreams as well as show appreciation. Good-rewarding procedures *reinforce* the work we do for God. Good rewarding is a form of teaching and value education.

Rewarding builds relationships on at least four levels:

1. Recognition encourages even closer ties to the ministry of the church.
2. Sensitive rewards result in bonding for the task team itself, creating the "we" feelings which give a further sense of satisfaction to persons who work together.
3. Unity within the church is facilitated as the purpose of the church is related to the work of its task groups.
4. Special recognition of leadership creates interest, and potential leaders may observe the satisfaction of accomplishment and want to join in Christian ministry.

Proper rewarding *motivates* and *remotivates.* At its best, rewarding is not just a payoff. Rather, it is positive, spirit-building communication.

Demotivation: Punishment in the Church

The focus of this chapter has been positive sources of energy for voluntary leaders in the church. Actions also occur which depress commitment and energy levels. The subtle forms of punishment employed when individuals do not behave as leaders desire can be sources for the reduction of energy flow from church members.

Some years ago a church struggled with opening the first integrated day-care center in the state. The decision-making process had been healthy, but the issue was so hot that pain and separation had come for some—even between old and trusted friends.

Following the decision to begin the center, Gene Marshall, the educator in the church who had initiated the effort, was called to the office of a key opponent, a prominent banker in the city. Gene was praised for his good work in the church prior to his interest in the day-care center. He was told he had a fine future until this decision and was reminded of the low balance in his checking account.

The banker then made an offer to help build a separate building for the black children. At a moment of truth in the conversation Gene told the banker, "I'm sorry, Mr. Hubbard, I can't do what you want because I am more afraid of God than I am of you."

After dinner and a worried conversation with his wife, Gene received a call from Mr. Hubbard who apologized and asked, "What does God have to do with this? I thought," he went on to say, "this was some crazy sociological experiment they taught you at the seminary." Gene discussed with him the religious significance of the issue, and the banker declared he did not want to be opposed to the church's obedience to God. He said he would resist no more and went on to ask if Gene would call the pastor for an appointment the next morning at eleven o'clock.

With joy in his heart, Gene called the pastor, and the appointment was made. The next morning the three met in the pastor's study. The banker told his story, asked to be forgiven, and promised not to resist the day-care center anymore.

The pastor refused to accept the request for forgiveness or shake hands with the banker. He simply stayed behind his desk and said, "We'll see!" For the next several years the banker was not allowed by the pastor to have a role of leadership in the elected or organized life of the church. *Punishment?!*

This issue can be dismissed by our need to deny it exists in the church. We don't like to admit that there is a reasonably effective, unofficial, but highly visible punishment system at work in churches.

Do you need more convincing? The pastor and chairperson of the nominating committee meet and discuss key leaders. Members who are not viewed as cooperative are quietly omitted from the list. Later at the nominating committee meeting when one of these names is brought up by the group, or other "undesirable" names are mentioned, the pastor or other minister and leaders make a quick negative nod or drop their eyes, and the name is passed over.

Sometimes the church member being punished is argumentative or resistant to the goals of the leadership. Such individuals are not reelected to office. When we talk with church people about punishment, they are quick to identify a list of subtle punishment techniques. They are used by clergy and laypersons alike:

- Refusal to speak to offending parties.
- Withdrawal of budget support for the church.
- Refusal to renominate to elected positions.
- Dropping out of attendance.
- Withdrawal of friendship.
- Refusal to consult on important decisions.
- Lack of invitations to social events.

It would be wise for us to remember that because persons do poorly in one task group does not mean they are total failures. The first task is recognizing that leadership assignments should be based on more than agreement or popularity. If we hold to the concept of the priesthood of all believers, we accept that all Christians face God for themselves, reacting to that relationship in unique and equally authentic ways. Nowhere does that doctrine imply that everyone will have the same gifts or abilities. Unpleasant attitudes, different ideas, or unhealthy personalities must not incur punishment, separation, or isolation.

The Christian way is based on acceptance, love, and the belief that God's Spirit will take our differences and weave them into strengths. Working this way takes time. We believe it is worth it! When we lift high the common cause of God's kingdom, communicate well our specific tasks, recruit and nurture servants of God in love, punishment in the church is no longer acceptable.

Manipulation or Motivation: A Delicate Difference

Motivation energizes persons for Christian service. Manipulation depresses. The task of effective leadership is to motivate people to love and serve the God of history who is revealed in His Son Jesus Christ.

Most of the tools of good motivation are tools used by manipulators as well. They are affirmation, communication, common cause, personal satisfaction, duty, and sometimes guilt. There is a fine line between motivation and manipulation which is not always drawn by Christian leaders. We believe the line is drawn at the point of respect for others and the recognition of their freedom to decide for themselves what is best for them. Whenever we play God by claiming to know what is best for another person, manipulation of others will be the outcome.

Freedom and respect are the key words in the debate between motivation and manipulation. The greater our respect for those two concepts, the less likely we are to be guilty of manipulation in ministry. Respect for God's highest creation is at stake, for every person is capable of responding for himself or herself.

The more you infringe upon these two intrinsic values, the more manipulation reigns. Check it out! Christian motivators are excited about the ability of people to choose and cooperate. Manipulators are excited about what is to be done and at any cost. They never seem to sense that what they do is damaging. They are sure they are right. In extreme cases, they violate the image of God in their fellows. Eventually, their manipulation will turn a church to depression, low morale, and noninvolvement.

Energy for volunteer leaders is a fragile quality. So many elements contribute to stimulating interest, vitality, excitement, and involvement in the church. We believe you can be an energy generator to the leadership of your church.

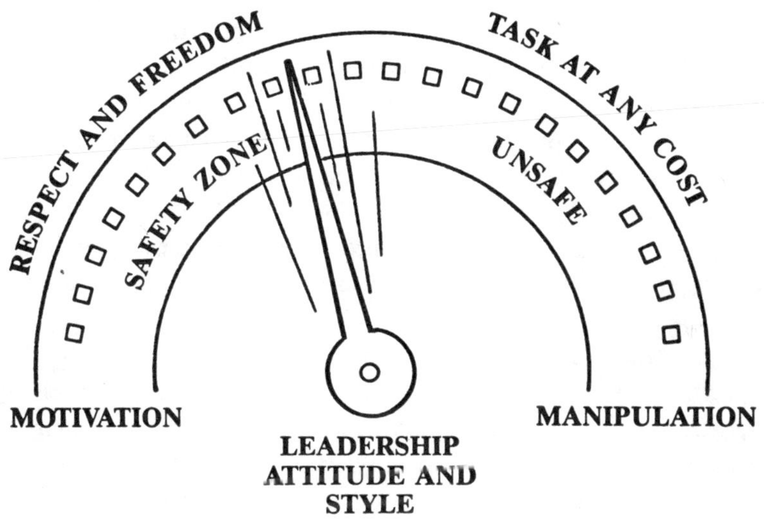

4
Nurturing Healthy Organizations

Effective church leaders usually want to be a part of a vital, healthy congregation. They will define health in terms of at least two important factors. First, strong church leaders will indicate they are committed to the growth of the church in some form. Their measurement of health is in terms of either qualitative or quantitative growth. Health implies vigor, strength, enthusiasm, and growth. Second, the way growth is defined is in terms of a symbol, motto, or phrase which is descriptive of the personality of the church. "We are a soul-winning church." "We want holistic evangelism." "We are the church where worship is central." "We are for quality growth with integrity." Each of these becomes a code word for a certain idea about the character of the church. Such code words and mottoes communicate what the church is about to newcomers.

Organizations are a means for communicating that personality. Now that we have seen how to birth a functional, healthy organization, and energize its leaders, it is essential to deal with the nurturing required to develop it into a mature personality. Beginning a new structure and developing one are two different kinds of tasks. In this chapter, we are concerned to focus on the practical needs for nurturing in healthy church organizations.

The nurturing task may require mottoes or code words as well. One of the mottoes Bill used to help his children work at their own responsible problem solving was: "*Look at it! . . . Think about it! . . . Work it out!*

From early childhood, our son Chuck had heard the motto. If

something was broken or not assembled, he was taught to look at it, think about it, and work it out! One day we were fishing from the boat, and Chuck had a backlash in his casting reel. Passing the rod and reel back to me he said, "Here, Dad, fix this for me, OK?" I chuckled and passed the rod back to him asking, "Chuck, what do we do before we ask for help?"

The memory I recall is of this eight-year-old boy holding the rod and reel with his knees, jerking on the backlash, and muttering, "Look at it" . . . (jerk on the line) . . . "Think about it" . . . (jerk) . . . "Work it out" . . . (jerk).

Churches work with the greatest health when they "Look at the tasks they have to do, think about how best to do them, and work out the most effective means of accomplishing them." Almost any task can be done with joy if we are convinced it is worth doing. Developing healthy, growing churches is worth the effort! Let's look at, think about, and work out how to nurture vital congregations.

Conduct Every Meeting with a Purpose

Healthy organizational development requires attention to the nitty-gritty of meetings. One of the primary reasons leaders are difficult to recruit is their past experiences with poorly conducted meetings. The healthy church gives attention to the leadership of its meetings. Every meeting at church should accomplish at least four things:

1. Affirm personal involvement in and commitment to the work of the risen Lord, our common cause. There is a distinctly spiritual dimension to the work of a church. It should be reflected in the meetings of the congregation. Thus, some appropriate attention to the Christian purpose of the meeting is in order.

2. Affirm each leader or committee member as an important part of the work of the church expressed in the task of the group. Team members must know each other and support each other. Recognizing the needs and contributions of the members is a must. At every point of a meeting, attention in a healthy organization is given to the personal needs of people, both those on the leadership team and the people the church is

called to serve. Early in the life of a leadership team the building of a community of trust is vital. This process is called "getting on board" or creating connectedness. As the group moves into its work, less time can be spent in community building.

A word of caution! The decision of how much time to devote to community building is a delicate one. Sometime ago, Lyman Coleman of Serendipity fame developed a chart that indicates community-building/taskwork balance. Coleman would draw a "ribbon cake" on the chalkboard of his workshops to illustrate this balance.

• *Slices* represent the meetings of a task group.

• *Time Allotment* for the meeting is a cross section of the cake.

• The hatched section marked *Community building* helps one envision the percentage of time used in this process. More time is used in the initial meetings, less time in the meetings to follow.

• Later in the life of a group community needs are not as great, and more time and energy are freed for the *task assignment* of the group.

Anytime the composition of a group changes, the community building

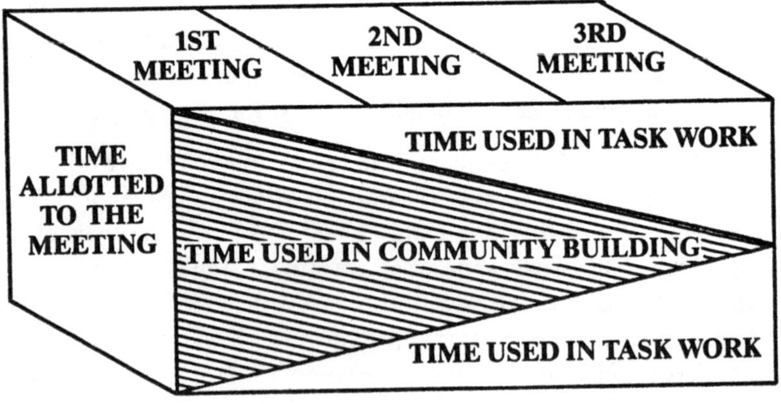

process will have to be reengaged. Rotating committees which add newcomers annually often continue the task work of the group without integrating new members. Recurrent absence of a group member has the same effect. The beginning of each meeting can be a time of checking up on the trust level and bringing all members into an awareness of what the group has been doing. Remember, as important as the task is, our first assignment is to love people—*especially those on our leadership teams.*

3. Convene around a prepared agenda. Each meeting should have a clearly stated time frame adequate for the items to be considered. If regularly scheduled meetings exceed two hours in length, the frequency of meeting or the presiding practices of the chairperson should be examined. Most church meetings are conducted at the end of the workday. People are often tired, have not had the opportunity to be with family, and can become irritable. Often the chairperson is retired, unemployed, or employed part-time. A three-hour meeting may not be stressful to that person but will be for the busy member.

Experienced meeting leaders soon learn the dynamics of how groups decide. Most groups will utilize all of the time allotted to them for whatever task is at hand. If the amount of time available for an agenda item is stated initially, most groups will work more efficiently to complete their tasks in the allotted time.

A second dynamic of meetings is that the first item of agenda receives the most attention and time. How often have you participated in a meeting when three fourths of the time was spent on unimportant matters while a most critical decision was settled in a few minutes because the time for adjournment had come? Wiser decisions can be made if the most important items are scheduled first.

Include time at the conclusion of the meeting for reviewing what has been done, making assignments, and concluding. Nothing is more frustrating to a leader than to have half of the committee begin leaving before there is any closure for the meeting.

4. Celebrate the work done at the meeting and the fellowship enjoyed. Some form of closure which emphasizes the good feelings and productive

work of the group needs to be included in the agenda of the healthy group.

Manage Groups with Efficiency

Support is both personal and organizational. A part of the support work of a good leader is efficient management. The first time the two authors of this book met they clashed over efficient management. Larry was a committee member in the church where Bill became a new staff member as educator/administrator. Larry was angry because the work of the committee had been rejected by the deacons of the church. He dumped his anger on Bill. Instead of reacting defensively, Bill responded constructively with a promise to ensure efficient management. Trust flowered in that experience. A friendship emerged that has now lasted ten years. Good management is also good support.

Some hints for management with
those busy and valuable
people who agree
to work in the
planning and
project life
of the
church.

1. *Give plenty of lead time!* The people who lead in the work of the church are usually already very busy people. Their time is valuable to them. The nature of the volunteer work in the church has changed drastically since World War II. In the 1950s, according to Daniel Yankelovich, "A typical American family consisting of a working father, a stay-at-home mother and one or more children constituted 70 percent of all households."[1] Thus, the homemaker mother was available to volunteer time and energy to church work without pressure. By 1980, this pattern of family described only 15 percent of American households. Volunteers for the church now consist of working men and women, retirees, and a few homemakers. Only in the most affluent churches is the nonemployed female a significant source of volunteer assistance.

What the church gets from volunteers today is *discretionary* time. This time is sought by many rivals in an age of increased volunteerism in the nation. It follows then that people must feel that the time they spend in church is a good investment—time that produces satisfaction and certainly not frustration. This is especially critical in urban churches.

A meeting worth asking busy people to support is one worth preparing for in every sense of the word. The "laid back" leader who wants to wing it on personality or the laissez-faire leader who expects someone else to do the work will anger busy volunteers. That anger will be shown by nonparticipation in the next meeting.

Want to have participation in your next meeting? Then, give your group written notice at least ten days before a meeting. If it is the first meeting of a new group or a critically important one, telephone each member the day before the meeting to remind them and encourage participation. Include the purpose of the meeting and a list of ideas and concepts each member might want to consider before coming together. Be sure the notice includes the basic time and place, *including when the meeting will adjourn.*

This last item cannot be overstressed. In this hustle-and-bustle world, leaving on time is as vital as starting on time. Expecting persons to stay overtime to work on an unplanned, disorganized meeting results in a domino effect of inconvenience and stress building. The aftermath is: frustrated baby-sitters, worried children and spouses, disrupted plans, and the erosion of members' morale. Announce when the meeting will end and plan to finish on time.

2. *Have a clear statement of purpose.* Write the purpose of the group's task on a flip chart or chalkboard before the meeting and put it in a prominent place in the room. This highly visible statement will help every member feel more comfortable and confident about the tasks to be done. It can also be used by the leader to call the group back to its purpose if the meeting begins to stray from the agenda.

Findley Edge emphasizes this point in a beautiful way as he teaches about Sunday School lesson aims. He says, "If you can't be specific enough about your lesson to write it down, you are not ready to teach the lesson!" The same truth applies to meetings. Let's paraphrase it: *If you can't write down the specific purpose of your meeting, you are not ready to meet!*

3. *Develop a preplanned agenda.* On the flip chart (below the purpose of the meeting), place a time line and an agenda. If the church has secretarial staff, a printed agenda may be useful. The adoption of the agenda should come early in the meeting. After opening the meeting with prayer, give each group member an opportunity to respond to the plans for the meeting. Items of importance may have been omitted. Other issues may have emerged since the last meeting of which the leader is unaware. The adoption process serves two important functions: (1) it focuses the best insights of the group on the work to be done; (2) it gives the group ownership of the tasks before them.

4. *Choose the best meeting place.* Most church meetings are conducted in the evening at the end of tiring days or during weekends when people are relaxing at the conclusion of a busy week. Thus, a comfortable meeting place is important. A room which is well ventilated, easily accessible, with well-lighted and safe entrances is important. More and more churches are doing their meeting work in the homes of members. This promotes a time of social interaction and often reduces travel time to the church.

The size of the group is important in how the room is arranged. A larger group calls for a more formal seating arrangement, a central place for the leader, and a more-structured agenda.

Feelings Are Always a Part of the Agenda

Since feelings will always force their way to the top of any agenda, we must teach people how to handle feelings responsibly on leadership teams. This is difficult in our culture since we have been taught to deny our hurt, anger, and frustration; some even call such denial *Christian.* This kind of denial is not only unchristian, it is unhealthy. The solution to the denial problem is not destructive ventilation or total exposure of feelings. Rather, identifying, owning, and appropriately expressing angry feelings are the means to healthy teamwork.

For the past few years, we have used a process outline for the responsible identification and handling of feelings in our Conflict Ministry

Seminars. It is not original, but we do not remember its source. Since feelings are always part of the agenda, leaders must learn to identify their feelings and help group members identify theirs. We have been helped by recognizing the varying intensity of feelings in a group. The following diagram indicates how the intensity of feelings grows as it becomes evident and of more concern to persons in a working group.

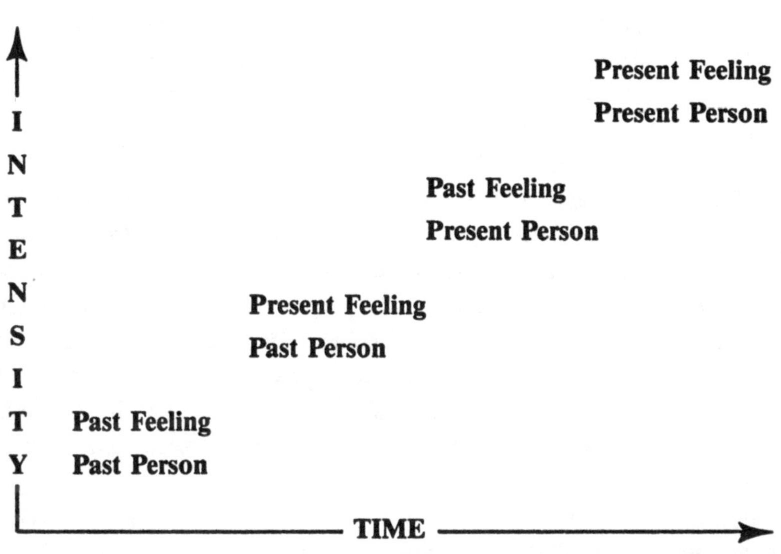

Intensity of Feelings in Task Groups

As long as the feelings in a group remain in the past, they can be managed rather easily. The threat of expressing feelings grows as they become focused upon current issues and persons in the group. When negative feelings emerge within a task meeting, assist the members in discussing what is happening. The leader can ask, "Why am I feeling uncomfortable? Angry? Cynical? Fearful? Hopeless? Or even bored?" The leader in charge must beware of the avoidance tendency and early cultural conditioning toward his or her own feelings. The feelings in a group must be claimed. "This feeling is mine, I feel fear or hostility," or "I am a Christian and still I'm feeling ________ tonight!" Patient leaders will often engage in ownership of feelings by engaging internally in self-talk. "I, James Hendricks, a Christian, am jealous and a bit afraid of Harold Springfield as chairperson. This feeling affects how I am reacting to what he is saying." We think it is better for our leaders to identify and own their feelings than to find themselves speaking impulsively or behaving negatively.

When the process has been followed to this point it is time for the leader (who knows what his or her feelings are) to deal with them in a constructive way. Constructive action has a positive effect upon the group. One way may be simply to spend a few moments talking it through with the group. Perhaps a members's feelings are too intense for the group to handle at the moment, and a private conversation with the leader would be better. If the feelings are not resolvable in this way and remain so intense as to be harmful to the group, seek help from a responsible outside source.

Beware of the weight emotions put on every agenda. It is much easier to handle feelings if the leadership team builds "feeling checks" and permission, even encouragement, to share into the process of work. Training of a leadership team in the first few meetings will facilitate this encouragement and permission.

Bill experienced a way to do this when working with a new task group. After the first few meetings a wastebasket was placed on the floor in the center of the room. Negative feeling checks were discussed, and the team members were taught to toss a ball of paper at the basket when they were aware of negative feelings making an impact upon their work. The movement of the paper in the air, the "basket," or "miss" got everyone's attention, and the feeling report was made. Bill made the first toss at the basket after the group was at work. Everyone did look up; some laughed and teased about his missing the basket and his obvious football background. He then said, "You know, about ten minutes ago I made a specific recommendation about how we might do our work, and you made no response. I'm feeling left out." They then talked about his feeling and one of his suggestions. For the rest of the evening, people who wanted to put out a feeling report threw their paper at him in a playful way. The entire group loosened up and worked at their task in a way that allowed them to deal with their feelings.

This story implies some significant possibilities for unresolved feelings. If a person continues to feel ignored, she usually chooses one of two negative responses. One is to drop out . . . by leaving the leadership team or project. The first indicators are lateness to the meetings, then absence, and finally withdrawal when the behavior is challenged. Or, the unhappy team member becomes aggressive and belligerent. If there seems to be no nice way to be heard or to feel safe, people get tough, aggressive, and rude. Give the group permission to deal with feelings. They are a very real part of the agenda.

Consensus Is the Best Way to Decide

It is our conviction that one reason for much unresolved conflict in churches is the way decisions are made. Organizational groups vote too often and too quickly. Have you ever wondered why some leaders vote one way in committee and another way in the congregation? Aside from all the uncomplimentary thoughts we have had about their courage and character, what really happened? We do not believe that they intended to mislead the church or to send double signals, nor do we believe that they talked to a spouse and got their "real" instructions. It seems obvious the group was not ready to vote. These members were not finished with the decision-making process. The vote is second-guessed, weakening the task group's morale and enthusiasm. Consensus is a much better way to decide many issues.

Consensus process moves a team toward a goal and will keep leaders aware of when or if they should vote. Consensus means having agreement on the directional mood and mind of the group as stated by a group member. The group does not vote with the majority winning. Rather, the group simply agrees with or modifies its thinking for the moment. A consensus statement might be accepted even though one or two would object if asked to vote. They agree in consensus with the opinion of the larger group.

Let's try it.

Suppose Tom says, "I feel the group is ready to recommend the purchase of the Ford property and that we need much more information on alternatives for financing the project." A person could be in the group, not wish to purchase the property, yet agree that Tom has read the attitude of the group. The consensus statement allows the group to gather information about financing without the pressure of a premature vote or a win/lose situation.

As the task process moves forward, members do not have to choose sides to take stands. They can reason together and demonstrate that six or seven Christians often make better decisions than the "Lone Ranger" leader asking for support. A large percentage of our task group decisions can be made by consensus and timely reporting. We are aware that every decision is not to be completed by consensus. Some actions must be taken by vote because of church and/or civil law. The greater and clearer our common cause, the easier it is to arrive at a consensus. Consensus spirit is better than legalism for building community and completing a task through enlightened leadership.

Evaluation in Light of Goals Is Crucial

The staff of a prominent church uses an evaluation notebook to help the staff and congregation set and meet common expectations. A *Peanuts* cartoon is pasted on the first page. Snoopy is digging a hole, and Lucy asks him what he is doing. Snoopy replies with glee, "I'm digging for gold!" "There's no gold in these parts," she replies. Snoopy smiles and replies, "Then I'm digging for diamonds!"

How often have we done just that? It's so easy to change our goal to fit what happened. Snoopy was at work. He would take what he found and declare the digging a success. Have you ever heard yourself saying, "Well, our revival really turned into a renewal effort. We did not have many decisions, none public, but we heard great preaching and singing. The spirit was sweet." These are worthy achievements. Goals worth accomplishing. But why did the church first plan a revival? Why is it that only twice in all our years in the ministry have we seen a project or committee effort reported as a failure? Is it because we usually do something good when we come together? Another and far more serious reason is that we are masters at drifting or shifting goals to fit the results. *Whatever happens is what we wanted to happen.*

We know of a church staff that set up discipleship training classes, used the best teaching team it could muster, and wanted the class members to develop a greater awareness of the call of God in their lives. The goal was to help the class members get in touch with their personal and spiritual gifts, putting those gifts into service in the church and community. Noble goals. The history of this project reveals that of the five classes, three have refused to be separated from one another. These three groups produced few leaders and little influence for God in the church or the community. The inward journey was primary; call and service were not. Rather than evaluate the group in light of the original goals, the leaders and church staff proclaimed this to be a valid way to begin and build new Sunday School classes. For groups to love one another and want to remain together is not unusual. To shift goals, however, is to leave the church without the hundred sensitive, service-oriented leaders it intended to develop.

Good leadership will develop the courage and skills to evaluate work in light of the set goals. Goals must be inclusive and yet, as we stated in chapter 1, must be achievable and attainable. Long-range goals are a must for healthy church organizations. To achieve them every group will need short-range goals on short time lines for its own morale.

It is difficult for leaders who are rotating off a team to transfer to others history, enthusiasm, energy, and pertinent theory information when they leave. Short-range goals put on a sensible time line help the group know where it is going. People need to evaluate in light of the goals they set. They need to wrap up the loose ends that accompany every task and celebrate, even when there is much more to be done in the long-range task. *Avoid drifting from goals missed to goals claimed with hindsight.*

Use Appropriate Parliamentary Procedures

Effective nurturing is needed for the larger decision-making groups of the church. Frustration is the result of work when committees to do their work well only to have their recommendations rejected in a poorly conducted business meeting. An important nurturing task is to plan for healthy business sessions for congregational meetings.

Most churches state formally they conduct business according to Robert's *Rules of Order,* but informally, they follow their own rules of decision making. This is fine as long as decisions are unimportant or have little disagreement. But in times of tension, formal processes are needed for healthy decision making.

The first nurturing step for business sessions is the choice of a moderator. A person who is respected by all segments of the church, who knows parliamentary procedure or is willing to learn it, one who will use authority to maintain control and who will be fair in presiding is essential. In our experience, incompetence in conducting a business meeting is a major source of organizational conflict. Fairness and respect can be easily lost by an unprepared presider.

The second nurturing action leaders can offer is training in parliamentary procedure. If voting is the process of deciding in the church, formal processes of voting should be followed in making trivial decisions so the group will know the rules in making major ones. Seldom will the most complex features of parliamentary procedure appear in a church. But the elementary matter of making clear motions and dealing with them according to stated rules will ensure fairness when the going gets rough. Appendix 2 contains a summary of parliamentary procedure which can be helpful to churches in making decisions.

The wise moderator will use each church business session as an opportunity to train the church in the rules of parliamentary procedure. By helping church members word their motion appropriately and recognizing them in the proper order, the church will learn healthy means for handling the difficult business session.

Communicate! Communicate! Communicate!

The last emphasis we want to make in nurturing strong and vibrant organizations is the importance of effective communication with the larger church community. Most task groups must be able to let others know their needs, ask for support, and communicate activities they are planning. We make several assumptions about communication in the church:

1. Assume that whenever an organization communicates a message, it did not get through to the intended recipient. At least 70 percent of the messages in the typical church are never heard.

Redundancy is required if you want to be heard. The greater the variety of messages about a given event or need, the more likely it will be heard. Thus, the effective organizational leader will work hard to understand all the media for communication—newsletter, Sunday School classes, posters, pulpit, and telephone. The more important the message, the greater the need for redundancy.

2. Assume that if the message did get through, it was garbled and not understood. Communicators too often think if their message is clear to themselves, it is clear to others. Such is not the case. Thus, the more people participating in the sharing of the message, the more likely it can be heard by the variety of the congregants.

3. Assume that receiving and understanding the message does not imply consent. Have you ever had the experience of asking, "Heard about the clean-up day at the church building this Saturday?" only to be told, "Yes, and it's marvelous we are getting together to shape things up." Then when nobody shows up to clean, you wondered what those conversations meant. Unless there is a commitment to what you are asking, the communication task is not complete.

4. Assume that two-way communication is superior to one-way com-

munication. Church organizational leaders can use several techniques for allowing others to participate in the communication process. Whenever you involve those beyond the organization in what is being done, greater commitment is likely. Surveys of attitudes, small-group dialogue, talk-back sessions, and systematic visitation are programmatic ways to secure two-way communication.

5. Assume it is easier to achieve communications within an organizational unit than between organizational units. Whenever the message must be delivered outside the structure originating it, the task grows in complexity.

Conclusion

Nurturing church organizations is a time consuming but meaningful ministry of the Christian leader. Ministry does not just happen. It emerges as the people of God give themselves in the tender tasks of loving the organism we call *church.* Persons do not grow without nurture. Neither do churches. But when they have been developed, the results are mature bodies which fulfill all the functions God intended of His community of saints.

5
Organizations Cry, Too!

"I have never been so humiliated in all of my life!" Ginger Thompson was not hostile as she told her story to the church conflict consultant helping her congregation. She was speaking softly, and tears were dripping from her cheeks as she described the church business session of the previous week. "All I did was move to table the recommendation of the deacons so we could have more time to think and pray about what we were doing. Then, after the meeting José Hernandez came up to me as mad as could be and said no true Christian would do what I did. He accused me of trying to run the church and refusing to cooperate with the deacons. He thinks I am some kind of women's libber who wants to challenge the men in the church."

Conflict is a fact of organizational life. Sometimes it is too painfully a fact of life. Organizations are made up of people, and they will experience the same pain as the people within them. Just as people sometimes cry, so do organizations.

We do not propose to explore all of the dimensions of conflict in this chapter. Several well-developed guides are available for church leaders' use in managing conflict.[1] Our aim is to focus on some practical suggestions for responding to organizational conflict.

Recognize the Signs of Conflict

Anticipation is the key to effective conflict ministry. When organizations get in the deepest trouble, it is often the result of failure by leaders to recognize conflict early enough. There are signs of conflict. Learning to read the signs of conflict is as important for the church leader as traffic signs for a new driver.

The first sign is the exit sign. Some people will withdraw whenever conflict occurs. They will exit first from the place where the conflict is most evident. If there are tensions with the pastor, the exit is first noticed in worship. If a committee has become dysfunctional, participation will decline. If decisions involving money are conflict producing, withdrawal of financial support will begin. The first sign of conflict is the exit sign.

Another exit sign is lack of interest in committee meetings. When those who have started a project with the group wane in dependability or become erratic in attendance, signs of a change in spirit and attitude are communicated. A spin-off of the erratic attendance syndrome is perpetual tardiness. Being late is often more than a bad habit; it is a statement of declining interest.

The second sign is the caution sign. Whenever cautious response is noted in the group, the potential for conflict is growing. This particular sign surfaces in response to change. The good conflict minister will anticipate that caution accompanies any new idea, new ministry proposal or alteration of patterns of functioning. *Change* is the trip word of much conflict.

When Bill was a high-school football player in Trenton, Tennessee, the team played an arch rival from Jackson, Tennessee. For Bill it was an important game. He had grown up in Jackson, gone out for Junior High football there, and was captain of a 2A Trenton team that had a chance to beat 4A Jackson High.

The score was zero to zero in the fourth quarter, and Jackson's quarterback called a deep reverse. Bill broke through on defensive tackle and was driving the Jackson quarterback deep into his own backfield for a loss. The two were in the open, and the crowd was on its feet in excitement. Trying to get more speed out of his 287-pound body, Bill tripped and fell. The announcer yelled over the loudspeaker, "Trenton's tackle tripped over the chalk line." The crowd roared in laughter. Trouble had come because he had tried too hard.

Change is the chalk line of organizations. They often stumble and fall at the most inopportune times. When we think all is going well, remarkable events take place. Some people speak of this in personal and theological terms: "The devil got hold of our people." They use the argument that the closer we get to the goal God has for us, the more trouble we can expect from God's opposition.

Others will say that it is a systems or psychological problem. When pressure is experienced, people respond out of their anxiety whether at work, home, or church. The longer the period of pressure, the more likely conflict will occur.

Finally, there are those who see trouble in the church as a management failure. Management by objective goals were either unclear or not fulfilled.

There is some truth in each of these positions, but we would also suggest that change is a primary dynamic in conflict. This is the chalk line that trips most organizations. Many deny their fear of change but have learned to cope with church life as a routine. Whenever the routine is upset, caution emerges in the form of silence, questioning, or gossip. Caution should be anticipated as the reaction whenever:

—A cause becomes too radical.
—The cost of a decision is considered too great.
—The commitment demanded is too extreme.
—There will be others who disagree.
—If the change is too much, too soon.

Change is a major key to the tension in committees and organizations.

Spirit is also a caution indicator. When the spirit of "we can't" or "they won't" replaces the spirit of "we could" or "let's try," a negative spirit is taking control. At times the only difference in whether a group makes progress or moves backward is the spirit of the group. We need to be aware of the birth and growth of the negative spirit, identify its sources, and find ways to change its reality.

The third sign of developing conflict is the detour sign. When churches turn away from their dreams and goals, conflict is likely. Churches who call pastors totally different from their heritage, install programs inconsistent with the past, or make quick decisions without careful work will experience conflict.

The fourth sign of conflict is the stop sign. Whenever rigid resistance to leadership appears, conflict is happening. The pastor presents a program that is rejected, committee recommendations are stymied in deacons' groups or Church Councils, or the suggestions of newcomers are dismissed.

The fifth sign of conflict is the U-turn. The reversal of positions between meetings, any behavior that is polarized in one direction at one meeting and shifts radically at the next are clues that confusion prevails. In these cases stress is usually high and conflict is intense.

Finally, "delay in traffic" is a sign of potential conflict. When a group or individual will not complete assignments, problems in the process may be indicated. Unclear or unrealistic assignments, personality or personnel problems, or an interpretation of the task as "busywork" contribute to this sign. Whatever the cause, there is conflict potential in legitimate work left undone over a period of time. We need to learn to spot the potential of conflict in unfinished agendas.

We'll call him Charlie. Charlie had a car dealership in a Southern town and was actively involved in the church. He and the ministerial staff were

CHANGE IS THE CHALK LINE!

together regularly planning training programs for the church members. He spent hours at the church giving time and energy to his task. He was young, hardworking, and ambitious.

But Charlie started to miss the Church Training planning meetings and Church Council meetings. His absence was a radical change. When his name was mentioned, the people in the group seemed uncomfortable. They became more and more negative. The education leader in the church became concerned and prepared to find out what was going on with the group. Before he could do so, however, the newspapers published a story stating the state revenue office was placing charges against Charlie and his auto dealership. What added to the tension was the presence of the state revenue prosecutor in the church. The conflict potential had been telegraphed by Charlie's behavior. A quicker response might have allowed the church to be a better minister to Charlie in the time of his distress.

Act to Prevent Unhealthy Conflict

When signs of conflict have been observed, they call for a response. We believe much conflict could be avoided if potential conflict were engaged before it emerged. We call this activity of responding to conflict potential "avoidance with integrity." The point is that harmful effects can be avoided if action is designed to respond to emerging conflict.

There are a number of possible strategies for handling emerging conflict. Active listening is one. Sitting down with the people for whom conflict is emerging and listening is a way of collecting information. Guidance can then be offered in the midst of what is happening.

A second procedure for dealing with emerging conflict is to correct problems in the organization. Suppose a task or goal is encountering resistance. A willingness to adjust and modify in light of new experience communicates flexibility. Problems can be expected when an approach to ministry is so inflexible that no change can be made once a direction has begun.

Summarizing and stating what is happening can be a good avoidance technique. Often the intention of a task is lost in the detail of doing it.

Task groups need help in restating their goals, where the group is in the process, and reviewing the next step in the process.

Pausing for refreshment can be an avoidance process also. Tasks need to be broken up with times of celebration, laughter, group building, and rest. Whenever a group becomes overly fatigued, it needs a change of pace and regrouping. A sensitive shift to relational concerns in the midst of heavy task work can relieve tension which may develop into conflict.

When Conflict Comes . . . Lower the Intensity

Unfortunately, one of the major problems in dealing with conflict is that we cannot control human behavior. In spite of our best planning, our efforts to avoid emerging conflict, and prayer for organizational success, conflict does come.

Speed Leas is the foremost consultant in church conflict today, in our judgment. He has outlined five levels at which conflict can occur.[2] We call these levels of intensity.

Level I conflict is the lowest level of intensity. It speaks of problems to be solved. Differences are real, but individuals focus primarily on the description of the problem, the causes which brought it to public focus, the importance of it, or the means for resolving it. Differences are not focused on group struggle, competition between leaders, or the possibility of solution. Feelings may be intense with flashes of anger, but not long-lived. Participants in the conflict believe it can be resolved through mutual discussion and problem solving.

Intensity Level II introduces opportunity for differences in a group to become unhealthy. At this level the conflict is manageable but may grow in intensity if the group is not led to a Level I style of coping.

The first evidence of the formation of power struggles among individuals is evident at Level II. Seeking to become a winner replaces the motivation of finding a solution to differences. Thus, the way persons describe the conflict becomes more vague, more emotional, and more accusatory. Data is guarded, shrewdness emerges, and humor often becomes a weapon against opponents. The discussion is designed more to score an advantage than to seek a resolution to the problem at hand. Compromise will be called for at this level. Yet, there may be no clearly identifiable groups trying to win.

At the third level of intensity, conflict moves in a riskier direction. The potential for disaster grows as conflict intensifies. At this level, a contest between competing groups within the church moves into a win/lose situation. The primary question of the groups is "Who will win?"

Formation of parties is a clear indicator of Level III conflict. Each party is committed to its agenda and particularly to winning its agenda. However, the groups may not be clearly defined. The leaders are visible and evident, but one cannot always tell who the followers may be. This level of conflict can take a number of forms. *Debate* is one form and includes attempts to win the mind of the opponent. *Games* may develop at this level as the contest is highly exhilarating. The parties desire competition because they want to prove who is strongest. There is no desire to destroy the enemy but rather to demonstrate strength. When contest becomes a "fight," the object is to get rid of the opposition. At this point, Level IV conflict is present.

The language people use in Level III conflict is highly distorted. Descriptions of the problems in the church are exaggerated, important information is omitted, we-they language is strong, motives of others are assessed, and generalization occurs. It becomes difficult to get agreement between the parties as to the nature, causes, needs, or solutions of the conflict situation.

It is difficult for conflict at this level to remain impersonal. Causes become more important than people, and personal attacks are substituted for dealing with problems. The parties have difficulty relating to each other socially or informally. Emotion replaces rationality. Motives of opponents are described and judged. Disputes emerge over who initiates efforts for peace, and parties use the statements of opponents against them.

Most church people will identify conflict at Level IV as destructive and harmful. Usually, there will be a strong tendency for people to flee the conflict at this level. They either must join one of the parties or leave. This level is called Fight/Flight.

The primary characteristics of Level IV conflict are the desires to hurt, humiliate, weaken, punish, or destroy the opponent in the conflict. Most often this level in the church is evident in a conflict between the pastor and the congregation. The congregation is set against the pastor and not only wishes to get rid of their leader but may want to prevent him or her from serving as a minister in the future. Strong leaders of disciplined groups emerge in Level IV conflict. The focus of energy is on defeating an opponent rather than resolving the issues. Others' feelings become unimportant, and the idea of a division is not threatening. Conflict is personalized, motives questioned, and expulsion rituals practiced toward opponents. Opponents do not socialize with each other.

Conflict at Level V is rare within the church. When it does occur, responsible members must act quickly to prevent destruction of the witness of the congregation as a fellowship of Christian concern. When conflict at this level occurs, the parties cannot quit fighting even when agreements have been negotiated.

The major objective of Level V conflict is to destroy the other. It happens in families, communities, and occasionally in churches. Physical violence may be threatened. In the church, this destructive tendency often turns into an effort to prevent the pastor from serving another church. The aggressors often present themselves in larger-than-life terms. They have a role in some "eternal cause." Any means is considered acceptable to fulfill the divine end for which they fight.

It is not our intention to develop a complete guide to dealing with each of these levels of conflict. What the Christian leader can do in each situation is seek ways of lowering the level of intensity of the conflict situation. Healthy conclusions cannot be achieved if conflict, at whatever level, cannot be moved toward a Level I situation. This process of lowering the level of conflict once it has occurred and become public, we call *diffusion.* A number of diffusion strategies are possible including information gathering, trust-building exercises, encouraging maximum participation, teaching communication skills, allowing expressions of feelings, and stating ground rules.[3] Of these, we believe information gathering is the most important means of lowering conflict intensity.

Diffusion: Identify the Issues

Diffusion is taking place when a rational process of information gathering can be followed. At higher levels of intensity such as Level IV, this procedure will probably not be possible. It is our judgment that when a conflict reaches Level III and certainly Level IV, a professional consultant or denominational leader should be called in to assist the church. This is a procedure we have used successfully with lower-level conflict situations.

1. Select a comfortable room for discussion of the conflict issues. We avoid meeting in church sanctuaries or auditoriums. A room just large enough for the number attending with chairs arranged in a circle or semicircle is ideal.

2. Have available large pads of newsprint. Record all items on the print

and save them for future use. If you use a chalkboard, you will not have a permanent record unless someone in the group takes accurate notes.

3. Begin the meeting with a brief prayer. We discourage much focus at this point on prayer or devotion. Often in conflict, spiritual language has been used to enforce one view, and this may retard discussion. Your goal is to get a maximum amount of information from the participants about the conflict. Most people do not consider dealing with conflict a spiritual time.

4. Distribute a sheet of paper or note card to each individual and ask each to write their perception of the issues. Have each list no more than two issues. Your aim is to focus on the primary problems. If the conflict appears to be low in intensity, ask each to read what was written. If the group is tense, you may want to collect the information and read it yourself. Writing out issues gives every individual some input. In addition, it avoids dominance by the more verbal participants. Often the parties in conflict will use their verbal skills to control the problem definition.

5. At the top of the newsprint pad write: THIS IS THE ISSUE. Record each suggestion from the participants without comment. Then encourage conversation and add to the list. Control the conversation so judgments about the accuracy of suggestions are not offered.

6. List the "spillover" issues. The more difficult the conflict, the more likely a number of issues may be involved. Develop as long a list as possible. If there are a wide variety of issues, the level is probably low, and what the group needs is focus and consensus. If a few issues emerge which generate strong disagreements within the group, you are likely getting at the real issues. State the rules of discussion using them to control the discussion and to prevent attack of persons in the room.

7. Divide into small groups and allow every person in the room to add to the list and express feelings about what has been listed. This is a means of lowering the feeling intensity about the discussion. As the leader, you must set the tone for the meeting by maintaining a controlled and fair approach. If your anger level rises, so will the group's.

8. Have each group report their discussion to the larger group. Add any new items to the list.

9. Move toward a discussion of priorities. Ask the group to begin identifying what are the most important issues on the list. Allow free and open discussion.

10. Test the mood of the group. Ask how each is feeling. Try to get an assessment of how much anger, hurt, fear, and resistance are in the room. Ask, "Do you feel ready to begin deciding what we will do?" This is as far as most groups can go in a first meeting. If the process has moved quickly and the group is ready to move, continue by going to step 14. If not, go to step 11.

11. Review the process for the next meeting. Set a meeting time, agenda, review the rules, and assign homework. Bring all of the notes made at this meeting to the next meeting.

12. Conclude the meeting as one group. We emphasize ceremonies of closing and celebrations of accomplishment. A circle with the group arm in arm singing and praying together is a good way to close. Now is the time to emphasize the Spirit of Christ within the group and the importance of seeking the will of God in all church decisions.

13. Begin the cycle over at the next meeting, reviewing what has been done.

14. When all issues have been identified, start a new list. WHAT CAN BE DONE? should be the heading for this list. Ask for suggestions from the group as to the step that could be taken to respond to the issues at conflict. When specific steps have been identified, seek a covenant of willingness to attempt the suggestions. Feed suggestions into the organizational structure in ways that will result in decisive actions.

15. Conclude the meeting on a note of commitment and celebration.

You may discover that the group is unable to discuss the issues. A small committee with conflicting personalities within it may become immobilized by the people in it. Enlarging the group to include the Church Council or key leaders may help. This is another diffusion approach.

Delay may also be necessary. If the issues are so explosive that people are unable to discuss them at all, waiting can give the parties time to cool down and think about what is happening. Seldom does any given conflict in the church require an immediate conclusion.

Engagement: Choose an Appropriate Strategy of Response

Once the issues have been identified, whether clearly or not, those matters must be engaged. We call engagement what one does about a given issue at conflict. It is the action we take to deal with the situation. Another word for engagement is strategy. How shall we respond to this situation? That is our strategy. Speed Leas has again provided excellent guidance as to the strategies available to conflict ministers.[4]

The primary strategy for ministry in problem-solving conflict settings is *collaboration.* Collaboration is a proactive strategy of working with all participants in the conflict to arrive at a mutually-acceptable solution to the problem being faced. Collaboration requires that all parties to the conflict mutually define the problem they face, mutually collect any data needed for dealing with the problem, mutually search for options which may resolve the issues, and choose together a solution by consensus. The use of authority, outside intervention, or quick solutions to the problems are usually counterproductive and may intensify the conflict to higher levels. This strategy works best in those conflicts which can be moved to a Level I intensity.

A secondary strategy which may prove useful in Level I conflict is *support.* Support is a process of encouraging the participants in their problem-solving approach to conflict. Support is the strategy of choice for those not directly engaged in the conflict. Support may also have a proactive dimension in terms of building trust for consensus within a group. Conflict leaders will always work to ensure fairness for all parties in the conflict by supporting the voice of minorities, by increasing the power of the decision-making group, and by building confidence within the group for making their own decisions.

The primary strategy competing groups use in conflict at the second level of intensity is *persuasion.* Forceful communication of one's view, argument, use of logic, and appeal to rules are all evidences of competitive conflict. Use of parliamentary procedure to deal with conflict is a sign of Level II intensity. In genuine difference, however, the persuasive process ensures a loser. Persuasion works well as a strategy when the persuader is an authority figure who is respected by all participants, is perceived to have no self-interest in the outcome of the conflict, and can use persuasion to convince the group to collaborate. Appeals to larger concerns are often the tactics of persuasion.

Another strategy of engagement is *negotiation* or *bargaining.* It works best in higher levels of conflict, especially Level III or IV. Outside negotiators are often needed to assist a group to clarify its conflict and work out a process for resolution that will move toward collaboration.

Negotiation is a strategy of compromise. For negotiation to work, the conflict must not be a conflict in the values of the persons involved. All parties must be willing to seek some solution and have enough balance of power that one group cannot be defeated easily. Effective negotiators begin by negotiating a process for working on the conflict, then working at defining the conflict at the more comfortable levels of discussion. Each aspect of the conflict must be discussed and negotiated a step at a time. If a party to the conflict, you must be clear as to the nonnegotiable issues in the conflict.

Lowering levels of expectation regarding the outcome of the conflict may need to be considered in negotiation. Seldom are the parties to a negotiated settlement of conflict enthusiastic about the outcome. According to Speed Leas, "Solutions suffice rather than satisfy." The outcome is the best possible under the circumstances but will not be exciting to either party in the conflict.

Compelling or *force* will be the primary strategies of responding to Level IV conflict. In Baptist churches this requires the use of the authority of the church, namely voting, to deal with the conflict. Since the whole congregation is usually involved in the fight, division may be the outcome of this level of conflict. Minorities in a vote may have to leave the church.

Such strategies work only in those situations where the leader has authority, can demand compliance with the authority, and has some ability to monitor performance. Thus, one must focus upon some process of decision making in most Baptist churches when the fight has emerged. Often a special arbitration committee in which the parties to the conflict have fair voice can be a means of developing a process to lower the intensity of the conflict.

You should not expect much enthusiasm for any outcome of a fight. Morale is usually low, guilt is strong, and a sense of failure may be overwhelming. Trust is destroyed in Level IV conflict. It takes time to heal the wounds of fighting.

If the issues are less important than the relationships involved, the strategy of many at any level will be *avoidance, ignoring, accommodating, or fleeing.* These avoidance strategies can be effective when the parties are too fragile to handle the conflict, when the church needs a rest, when there is no power to change things, or when you really do not care about the outcome of the situation. Avoidance strategies seldom produce fruitful outcomes, leaving the church depressed and conflict continuing.

The primary strategy needed for Level V conflict is *force.* Action must be taken to prevent the antagonists in conflict to act against those they would destroy. The highest levels of authority needed must be utilized including calling the police, if necessary. The combatants must be separated and authority used to keep them separated. Offending parties should be expelled from the group if they persist in offensive behavior.[5]

Seek the Resources of the Holy Spirit

The most that is humanly possible when conflict comes is an agreement among the parties as to how they will deal with it. In the Christian community, there is a higher goal—reconciliation. But such a goal is not humanly achievable. Reconciliation is a gift from God which requires the work of the Holy Spirit in the lives of those in conflict. Such reconciliation calls for seeking the presence of God's Spirit in prayer. When conflict comes, it is time to pray. Thus, there is no time in the life of a congregation when the organizational leader needs to seek the resources of prayer more than in times of conflict.

Good can come when organizations cry. But it will not come automatically. Seldom will the good feel good at the time of conflict. But beyond the reality of the pain of hurt feelings, battered egos, frustration with immature people, downright stubbornness, and ordinary meanness, there can be the working of God's love among His people. The effective leader must be a person of prayer for the reconciliation of God to find its way as a gift to Christians fighting with each other.

Years ago, Bill worked on the staff of the Oakland Baptist Church in Rock Hill, South Carolina. The pastor of the church was Dr. W. L. Ball, Jr., who had served churches in South Carolina all his adult life. On one occasion they were visiting in the hospital together. Dr. Ball went to a hospital room he could not enter, so he placed his bowed head against the door and prayed for the patient whom he could not see. "If the patient were unconscious and alone, why don't you just pray for him from our study at church?" Bill asked Dr. Ball. In response, this mature pastor answered more than the question. "I want to get as close as I can for as long as I can. I love these people."

So it is in prayer for those in conflict. The leader has to love those who are at war with each other, including those who are enemies to the leader's ministry. Conflict requires power beyond our own if reconciliation is to come.

The Holy Spirit joins us in planning, dreaming, and even conflict management in organizations when they cry. God's presence is there for us when we are aware of it. We must want to get as close to God as we can for as long as we can. The same is true for the people of the organizations we serve. In God's Spirit we need to be as close to them for as long as we can if we truly love them.

God's Spirit will not only help us love more but will help others in conflict respond in openness and love. New channels are opened through prayer, sharing, and the common cause of mutual ministry.

Build a Nest Around the Group Decision

The way to test any conclusion to conflict is at the point of relational improvement. Are we able to work together more freely? Is there energy in the group to accomplish our tasks? If the answer is yes, then it's time to get back on course and work on our goals as an organization. If not, the conflict work is not completed, and we must go back to working the process we have outlined here. This is what is called the feedback loop. We must loop back to an earlier stage of conflict ministry and work the process again if we are to get back on track organizationally.

The final outcome of conflict will be rooted in a decision by the persons who have engaged it. Genuine reconciliation is manifested in a concrete act agreed upon by the fighters. That is what we mean by a conflict decision. Thus, concluding conflict is more than a cessation of hostile feelings. It is arriving at new patterns of behavior.

There are several different ways this can be described. We like to call this process "integration on a higher plane." By this we mean the group comes together with a higher sense of commitment to each other and to the work of God's kingdom than was obvious before the conflict. For such integration to occur, however, there must be new covenants, new decisions, and new commitments which bind the church together. There must be a nest-building process at work in the group. Conflict theorists call this "refreezing." It is the period of stability which must follow any period of major change.

Nest building must put the new conclusions to conflict back into the organizational structure. Agreements should quickly be written into

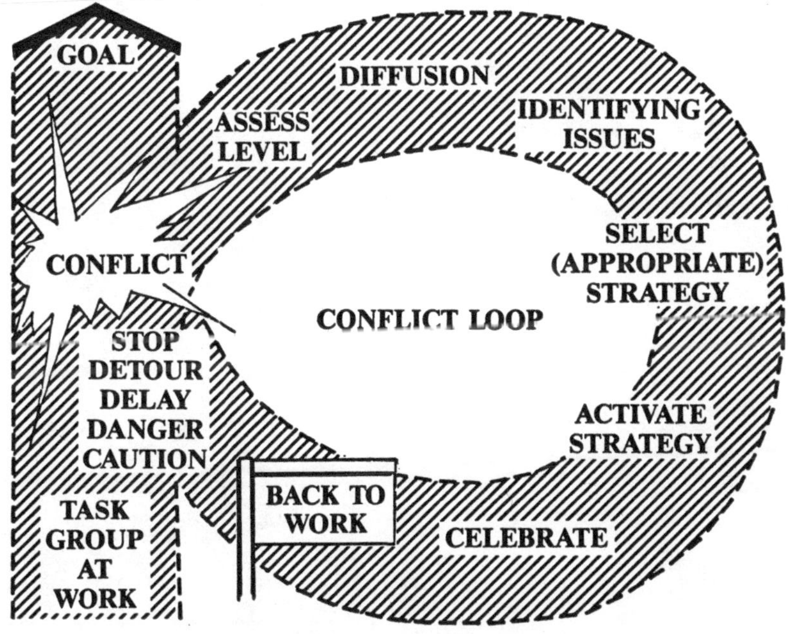

policies, bylaws, and procedures. Report the agreements as widely as possible through all media available in the church.

Nest building is also a "thank-you" process. Whenever an organization has moved through conflict, personal and public recognition of those who have contributed to the process should be made.

Finally, celebration is a time of nest building. Reconciliation calls for worship. The people gather to declare their oneness in acts of praise to the One who unifies when true integration on a higher plane has taken place.

6
Reinventing the Church

"Our church is just like me. Old and dying." Pain was evident in Walter Byrnum's face as he spoke the words. "We ought to go ahead and close it while we can. I can't stand the thought of watching it decline anymore."

"But Mr. Byrnum, some of us younger members would not be here if that had been your decision ten years ago," reacted Helen Wang. "We have never known this church to be big like you have. There are ten Asian members here tonight who experience this church as exciting and alive. We have dreams for this church. Let's not close it!"

"At least one third of the churches in our association are like us," John Meadows complained to the Church Council. "We are on the plateau while 40 percent are declining. These are the latest figures from our Home Mission Board. It's time for us to get back in gear. Why, our community is growing, but we are standing still."

"We need to do something to involve the younger women of the church in our mission's program," declared Helen Williams as she addressed her women's circle. "The only people who attend our circles on Tuesday morning anymore are the same faces. Ladies, our church needs the involvement of the younger women!"

"Yes, Helen, that is true," retorted Mary Cernak. "But we all know the younger women in this church work now, and they are not going to come during the day. My daughter says she is so tired at night she does not need another meeting to go to during the week at night."

"Maybe we ought to have our circle meetings on Saturday or even as a part of our Sunday activities," suggested Aline Douglass. "We need to do something to get some new life in this organization."

Any established organization must struggle with the inertia of its existence. Once set in motion, an organization has a life of its own. It is difficult to keep it dynamic and fulfilling a common purpose. Church organizations need constant renewal.

John Naisbitt, author of the best-selling book *Megatrends,* is one of the creative futurists thinkers of our time. His ideas for the renewal of existing institutions are expressed in *Reinventing the Corporation.* He suggests that society is in a process of unprecedented change from an industrial society to an information society. Every structure must somehow adapt to that fundamental social shift. His word for these structures is *corporation,* but he includes institutions like the church in his thought. Reorganized organizations are required within old structures if we are to face the future productively.[1]

Some of his ideas fit the church. Many churches have failed to adjust organizationally to their changing environments. Entrenched, declining, aging, and resistant, they find themselves frustrated with the sense of loss and decline which characterize their life. Churches are no more immune to organizational hardness than corporations. Thus, one of the principal needs within denominations and congregations today is the revitalization of old organizations into workable, vibrant, and exciting places of ministry.

Both of us work with local churches rather frequently to help them find a new sense of mission for the future. Larry worked with a congregation recently located in a neighborhood which had aged rapidly during the 1970s. Young couples were not able to purchase the expensive housing in the area, so the community experienced a rapid loss of young families with children. The local high school was closed. The elementary school suffered enrollment declines. The church became a group of retirees—talented, wealthy, but defeated because there were few young people in the church. They concluded there was no future for them.

I worked with them in a planning process to see if they could discover new ministry opportunities. What I found was that the people were fixed on what their community had been five years earlier. Already younger families were moving in again. Within the church was a small core of young adults on which a new future could develop. I began challenging them to dream about a new future. When I asked one group about their dreams for the future, one very attractive woman in her late fifties responded, "We are too old to dream." Mr. Roberts, at eighty the oldest man in the group, interrupted, "Julia, when you quit dreaming, you die. Nobody ever gets too old to dream. Why, I just bought a new car last week, and I intend to enjoy it!"

Every church has within it the resources for renewal. But they must be claimed. Naisbitt outlines three essential tasks for reinventing any institution. First, the leader must be the source of a vision for the group. If we were to apply his corporate language to the church Naisbitt would say, "We believe the first ingredient in reinventing the [church] is a powerful vision—a whole new sense of where a [church] is going and how to get there."[2] The primary responsibility of the leadership of the church is to provide this vision.

Second, the leader must attract people to share the vision and share responsibility for achieving it. Naisbitt calls this process "alignment."[3]

The third task for reinventing the church is to ground the vision in the daily operation of the organization. Lofty dreams take shape in specific tasks. Dreaming the dream is leadership, but fulfilling the dream is management.

Churches are not businesses. Corporate concepts cannot be sold wholesale in the church. But the concept of reinventing old structures for new purposes is essential if churches are to fulfill their mission under God. How they do that will be different from how corporations are restructured for more profitable results. Let's look at some practical ways of working toward the reinvention of the church in our time.

Dream Some New Dreams . . . But Not Too Many

The first task of reinventing the church is to dream a new dream of what it can be and do. Robert Dale has suggested nine stages through which congregations pass in their cycle of development from birth to death. The first of these is the *dream* stage when a congregation is born to fulfill a specific dream of its founding members. *Beliefs* shape this dream as the congregation develops a theology which identifies its uniqueness. Out of its beliefs, a church develops specific *goals* around which it organizes a *structure.* At some point in its life, the apex of its original dream is fulfilled as it accomplishes the *ministry* it intended. Then a decline cycle begins as the people lose their sense of commitment to the original dream. The first stage in the decline cycle is *nostalgia* as the people focus more upon the past than the future. *Questioning* follows as a search for answers to what has happened. Often a search for a scapegoat to blame for the decline is initiated. If the questioning continues, *polarization* results with unproductive conflict emerging. Groups crystallize and battle ensues. The final stage is the *dropout* stage as members begin to drift away to avoid the conflict of a polarized church. The church is inevitably weakened and sometimes dies.[4]

Dreaming is relatively easy for a church in the early years of its life and during the growth side of its life cycle. Here, the church is usually younger, more attuned to change, and more willing to do what is necessary to achieve the founding dream. Change is seen as creative and worthwhile.

Once a church begins the downward cycle, dreaming becomes more difficult. At the nostalgia stage, there is not enough dissatisfaction with things as they are to engage in creative changing. The attitude is often, "Let's just get back to the basics of visitation like we used to do, and our church will grow again." Efforts to reorganize may be viewed as premature, yet that may be exactly what the church needs at this point in its history. The earliest stages of losing vitality are the most important for making substantive adjustments to prevent deterioration. Yet resistance to change is often highest at this stage. According to Dale, the nostalgia stage is one in which there needs to be a reappraisal of the dream with a view to redefining the structures that used to work but need refinement.[5] In our experience, a change in leadership toward an aggressive, directive pastor is required to reorganize a church in nostalgia. Such an action often produces polarization.

The questioning stage is more productive for leading a congregation to a new dream. The depth of the decline in the church is more apparent. Tension has emerged, and there is the sense of impending crisis if something is not done. Churches will act and act decisively in the questioning stage. Often they act to replace the past only to discover that the problems they encounter are much deeper than pastoral leadership. Two facts are clear:

- Inertia or passivity are not options for a church in the questioning stage. The pastoral leader who uses a passive approach to ministry will find unhealthy conflict flowing as a result of standing still in the questioning stage. Action is necessary. It must be decisive. If not positive, it will usually lead to polarization. This is the time to plan, to bring in a consultant in new ministry possibilities, to inaugurate new ministries, and move the church off dead center.
- Radical change will polarize. The difficulties of renewing at the questioning stage are not a willingness to alter directions and structures, but attempting more change than can be handled. Since there is such an openness to make adjustments, the tendency is to attempt to restructure the church totally. Radical changes, even in an environment of openness to change, usually produce hardened resistance, conflict, and sometimes open warfare.

By the time a church has declined to the polarization stage, it will be open to attempt almost anything if it will promise the hope of survival. Churches attempt and complete unnecessary building programs, useless staff additions, and begin difficult ministries when they are desperate. Unrealistic dreams (fantasies) become the norm for this kind of church. The problem for the church which has experienced polarization is not that it is unwilling to work at change, but that it is so weakened it may no longer have the resources to achieve a new dream.

So what can be done to dream some new dreams?

1. Lead the church to a fresh study of the Bible on the mission of the church. Rev. Peter Sodeman is the only pastor the Morningside Community Church has ever had. Founded as a suburban mission in 1956, Peter became pastor of the small group of 40 people upon his graduation from seminary in 1957. Within ten years, the congregation achieved its initial dream. The church had a membership of thirty-two-hundred people, more than a thousand attended worship each Sunday, and the master plan for the facilities was being completed. During the eleventh year, the new sanctuary seating fifteen-hundred was completed. The only time it was ever filled was the day of the sanctuary dedication. Within six months, the first black family moved into the all-white neighborhood. Within two years the community was 10 percent black, and a small exodus of whites to the next ring of suburbs began. For nine successive years the church lost attendance until the congregation was down to 550 in worship attendance. Peter was still loved as the pastor of the church, but he lived in a state of depressed burnout.

In 1976, the church wanted to express appreciation to their only pastor and offered a six-month sabbatical to him. During this time, Peter began a fresh study of the nature of the church in the New Testament in a new environment. The stresses of everyday work were relieved. Slowly, a new enthusiasm for ministry and for the church he served began to grow within him. His focus was upon the church at Antioch. As he studied the Book of Acts he had a vision of the missionary church going forth in ministry to the people of a diverse culture. This was the vision for his church.

So he returned to the church renewed. Immediately, he began to teach the results of his new vision to the deacons in a weekly Bible study on Sunday nights. They caught his enthusiasm. Soon volunteers began to come forth to begin new ministries. The circle of study was expanded to the larger congregation and gradually the vision grew. Finally, at the end of six months of study the congregation adopted a new statement of their mission and inaugurated a new program of sponsorship for Asian refugees. The next year, two more ministries were begun. The third year saw three more ministries and a total reorganization of the committee structure of the congregation. Deacons became a servant group. Now the congregation has three ethnic groups worshiping in its building. Nearly eight-hundred persons worship weekly, but it is a new congregation of multiethnic and multiracial groups meeting in different parts of the building with a variety of leaders. The church was reinvented within six years.

2. Relive the original dream of the congregation. Often the story of the initial dream of a church is lost as newcomers join and children are born into a fellowship. Every new generation within a congregation must relive the identity of that church. Every congregation has within it the matriarchs and patriarchs of the past who can retell the lessons of the church's history to convey the hopes and struggles an earlier generation experienced. Have a heritage banquet. Videotape the oral traditions of the charter members or oldest members of the church for use in new member training. Write a drama illustrating how the church has lived out its dream in the past. Plan a homecoming. Build a celebrative worship event around the theme of the church's dream. Remember the past as a means of laying claim to the central theme of the church's mission. Then lead the church in a process of planning new goals for living the old dream in a new way.

3. Start a planning process and make its focus the future of the church. Sometimes a careful self-study of where the congregation is and what its directions indicate can be the means of reshaping trends. If the leadership of a church becomes aware of the nature of their decline and the options of new directions they can take, a new sense of purpose can be developed.

Pump Some New Blood into the Group . . . But Not Too Fast

New people are the best source of change in the inert church. Passivity becomes typical whenever the same group meets to do the same thing at the same time more than five times. Habit becomes the norm. But habitual practices do not attract newcomers who are not connected to the routines of a group. To alter passivity, one must change the group, change the meeting time, or change the meeting agenda. Routine is essential in the forming of a church or a group within it. You have to establish the routine of a regular format, at a safe place, with a stable group. But once a group is formed, it will tend to stay together and maintain its meaning by changing the place, frequency, and agenda of its gatherings. Callahan says a group will stay together for thirty-five years, once formed.[6]

1. Focus on new groups of young adults. The best source of new people is the myriad of young adults in our society who are unchurched. Unfortunately, churches have not been very good sociologists when it comes to reaching people. We tend to use the methods which attracted people best the last decade. But the tastes and needs of population within a community change from decade to decade. The largest single population group in our society is the age group born between the years 1946 and 1964. Whatever the age of this group, they will have a major impact upon the nation. When today's baby-boomers were infants, the churches were bursting with growth. When this group left home and churches during the college and early working years, many congregations experienced major declines. In the last decade many have reentered church life as their families were formed and children were born. By tailor-making ministries which meet the family, personal, and social needs of this age group, a congregation can begin a new future as it develops a new core of younger persons in its midst. As this group moves into middle adulthood, a rather different set of ministry needs will emerge to which congregations must respond.[7]

2. Rotate leadership. Another means of infusing new life into an organization is to identify new leaders who have new ideas and energy to offer the church. This is why the musing board idea in chapter 3 is so important. Nothing will create greater staleness than for the same people to repeat the same approaches year after year. In the stable and declining church, the same leadership has served in the same roles for more than ten years. Children of a dominating church member are often overlooked for leadership. Newcomers who have excellent experience in other churches but have not followed the traditions of the congregation are also ignored. Women with creative talents may be left out in the male-dominated congregation. Those who are quieter and less verbal

They have such great meetings, but it seems so hard to get into the GROUP -
BT 86

may be overlooked. Search for new leaders to involve in the work of the church.

3. Add staff. In some settings, the energy necessary for new vision must come from staff additions. In larger congregations the complexities of organizational leadership require full-time ministry and professional training. Too often the church overloads its staff to the point of burnout. Generally, a new staff person is needed for every 150 active members of a congregation if all their program needs are to be met.

4. Change job descriptions. One of the principles followed by outstanding leaders is to change jobs at least every five years. Sometimes that change occurs by staying in the same place of work but altering what is done and how it is done. Creative persons can continue functioning in the same roles, but only if they consciously work at maintaining freshness in their work. This can be done by the teacher who changes age groups, alters teaching style, redecorates the classroom, or begins writing the curriculum for teaching. The same leadership group might find renewal by assuming different roles in the small church, even though the same people are leading. A staff member in a role for more than five years needs the opportunity to redefine by adding new areas of responsibility, planning a reorganization of work, or supervising others.

5. Take a study leave. Fresh insight can also come into the organization by stimulating leaders with study opportunities. The healthy church will provide budget resources for lay leaders to share in short-term study conferences away from the church. Most denominations offer summer retreat conferences. Many seminaries schedule short-term workshops. Attend a special course in family education, evangelism, teaching, or missions offered by interchurch groups.

Resources should also be available for staff to participate in structured opportunities for continuing education at regular intervals. An investment in allowing fresh learning within a staff is a far healthier and less costly means of vitality than constantly changing staff.

6. Go on a mission trip. Another effective way to achieve change is to expose a worn-out group to fresh experiences. Even the most stable church can profit from the excitement of a new venture. A rural church can become involved in working in an inner-city ghetto during summer

vacations. A medical team sent to Haiti by a large urban congregation exposes people to new options for ministry in their home environment. Every church has untapped resources that may be used in exciting ways in another environment.

Stretch the Rubber Band . . . But Not Too Far

Changing a church requires more skill than negotiating a tightrope in a circus. One false step and it can be the end of the effort! All leaders suffer from the temptation of mediocrity by changing nothing. Yet, lethargy can be the sin which besets the contemporary church as surely as it affected the Laodiceans (Rev. 3:14-22).

The trick for change in the church is to balance pressure for change with support for the resisters to change. Kurt Lewin developed what is called a field theory for change. He stressed the fact that organizations never move toward an objective in a straight line. Rather, there is a series of up-and-down movements toward a change. These are caused by the pressures of opposing forces at work in any field of change.

Someone must be willing to stretch the rubber band. The agenda of change may sometimes be the force which raises questions, suggests alternatives, proposes new programs, or works for a new direction. There must be unfreezing of a situation in order for new directions to emerge. If there is no genuine need for change, it is best not to introduce actions which have the effect of altering the stability of the organization. How can change be introduced into the stable or dying church?

1. Study the bylaws. One of the ways change can be initiated is to review the formal documents by which a church functions. Since the bylaws represent the tradition of the congregation, any review is a process of opening up the potential for change.

Some driving force must be present, however, if change is to occur. The idea of bylaw review assumes dissatisfaction with present practices or some need within the church for a different method of functioning. Where the need is present, this can be a systematic and orderly means for opening up the possibility of formal changes in the way the church is organized or the way it processes its work.

2. Bring in a consultant. Outside specialists are also a means to change.

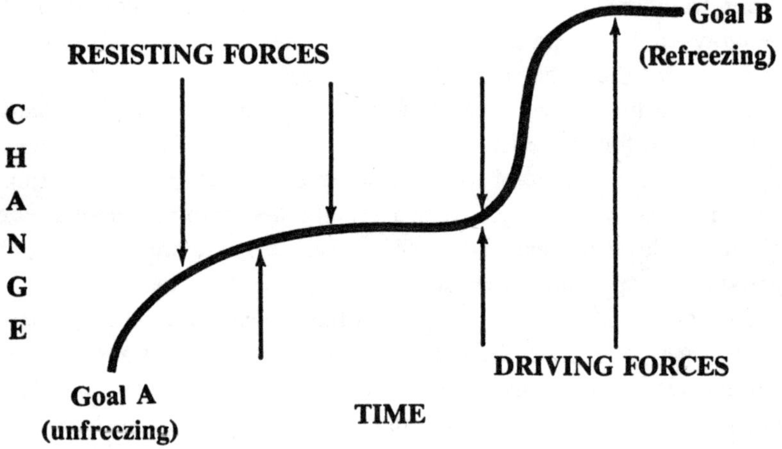

Field Theory of Change [8]

By bringing in an expert in the area of needed change, careful assessment can be made of the present ministry and the degree of support for change within the congregation.

3. Add staff. Adding personnel is an act of change. It stimulates

attention in an area of needed ministry, generates a greater commitment from church members for financial support, and adds another person giving focused attention to the work of the church.

4. Organize a visit of leaders to other successful churches with similar goals. A new experience of exposure to another congregation working in similar settings as yours can plan ideas for new ministry. It can also expose leaders to the energy needed for more effective functioning within your church.

5. Precipitate a crisis. Some situations will move off dead center only in the midst of a crisis. Threatening resignation, terminating staff members, replacing lay leaders, or introducing demands all have the effects of generating change. However, this is risky. The risk is that the crisis may generate so much conflict a pattern of flight from the church develops. It can also stimulate hostility toward the leader. Threats and precipitous actions can result in a decision to find a new leader! One can generate only one crisis in any five-year period of the average church's life cycle.

Stretching the rubber band is a driving-force strategy for change. One must recognize that change can also occur if the opposing forces lower the level of their resistance to change. In some situations the best change can be effected by developing caring relationships with the resisting forces and convincing them of the need for change. In most churches, this will be the most productive means to change in the long run. In the short term you may have to stretch the rubber band. But be careful not to break it!

Change is never easy for the church. As an ordering institution, the church is most effective at providing a tradition for people to live their lives with security. To upset tradition is to destroy the basis for church for many people. Yet, when a given tradition has outlived its usefulness in allowing a congregation to fulfill its mission, change is necessary. But once the change has occurred, it will require a refreezing to ensure its continuation. People cannot function in a vacuum. So whenever you change, you must build a tradition around the newly accepted practice or goal which may cause it to become rooted in the need for a future change.

7
Let's Celebrate!

The parents had gathered for the last service of an elementary camp prior to returning home. This service was to be a worship experience led by eight cabin groups. Each group was to conduct a tour of the campus and bring the parents to the concluding service prepared as a part of the week's worship workshops. The camp director wanted the service to model what the children had learned and to lead the participants in meaningful worship.

Each group had prepared the meeting place for its presentation. Everyone was there but the boys from cabin 6. This bunch was the rowdiest in the camp but the pets of everyone because of their liveliness. The director was worried. "Where could they be?" he wondered. Then he saw them climbing up the muddy creek bank at the edge of the camp. His anger grew with them and their counselor as they marched to the worship center covered in mud. They carried a huge leaf covered in mud and stretched between two sticks into the worship center and placed it on a stump they set up for an altar.

One muddy lad stepped forward and picked up a muddy doll. It looked like half a huge, gingerbread man. He grinned, his eyes sparkled, and he held up the mud doll. "He is only half finished," he said. "And so are we. He is not perfect because we made a lot of mistakes making him. We are not perfect. We want God to finish us 'cause He'll do a better job."

There was silence, then another little fellow led in a short prayer and a profound silence followed. It was broken when a tearful mother scooped up a muddy boy in her arms and swung him around in joy, laughter, and hugs.

And sure enough—a little child did lead them!

That kind of joy ought to be the consequence of our work in church organizations. Too seldom do churches celebrate together what they have experienced. We have come to experience that true joy in ministry happens best when there are planned opportunities to celebrate the presence of God in our work.

How? We have worked together for eight years and find we must build into the work times of relaxation and worship if our partnership is to be kept alive. Since we both love to fish, we try to find a fishing place at each work assignment. The fishing trips seldom help the food budget, but they add to the memory bank of good stories and expectations. These mutual work-and-play times give a sense of well-being, of belonging, and of joy in working in God's kingdom. Dinners, playtime, informal conversations, prayer together, worship, and social events are all celebration events. When a church staff or denominational staff group celebrates around a common theme with families, new commitment for the work together grows.

You have, no doubt, encountered the rigid, duty-bound brothers and sisters who will say, "Don't thank me, I did it for God," or, "Spiritual work is serious work. Cut out all the playtime," or, "We spend too little time on the important by having a social every time we get together." Some will even suggest the money and effort spent on celebrating would be better spent in more serious and spiritual matters.

What is meaningful celebration? We like the concept that celebrations are *ritualized interruptions* in the flow of daily living that remind us of who we are, where we come from, and where we are going. Ritualized interruptions need planning and effort. Consider the possibilities:

- Homecomings.
- Easter and Christmas rituals.
- Church dinners. In spite of the jokes about cold asparagus and paper plates, they can create family among strangers.
- Graduation events.

- Thanksgiving.
- Gathering in a circle to pray together.
- Parking lot conversations after church.
- Sunday School class parties.
- Fishing trip for the boy's mission group.
- Senior adult bus tour.
- Retreats.
- Picnics.
- Anything you can think of that sounds fun.

Appropriate celebrations communicate two dimensions of organizational ministry. First, they communicate what has happened to the folks who have worked together—a growing Christian commitment, reinforcing the importance of the task accomplished, deepening involvement in the church, closer friendships with each other, flowering of the Christian spirit, and emerging Christian relationships.

Second, celebrations communicate the nature of the faith of those who work together. As we celebrate, so we believe. If we feel life is good and God has blessed us, that spirit gets communicated as the bounty of God's grace to the world.

When Bill's family was much younger, they went to see the outdoor drama *Unto These Hills.* The story is a moving portrayal of the plight of the Cherokee Indians in North Carolina as they were sent to a reservation on the "trail of tears."

During the play, daughter Christy snuggled into Bill's arms and started crying. "What's the matter, honey?" he asked. "Why is it always us?" she answered. "What do you mean, Chris?" he asked again. "Why is it always the white person being so mean?" she replied. She was troubled, guilty, and needed help. Bill had no instant answer and waited a few minutes to reply.

Then the answer came in the play. A white Christian minister and his family decided to stay with the Indians and make the trail of tears their trail also. The minister was choosing to make the Indians his people. "See, honey, those are our people. Christians like them are our family," Bill said to Christy. The Christians in the play began to march and sing in celebration of their faith and fellowship, even in difficult times. The celebration was vital to the witness and spirit of the group.

There is an essential difference between this quality of living and secular reward. The secular reward system is based on the concept that we gain status and wealth as we perform. The norms of the groups in which we participate reward our contribution to that group. Thus, the professional football player shares in the victories of the team by receiving overwhelming amounts of money and watches, rings, pictures, and the right to be written in the record books. The bottom line of the secular reward system is: "Look at me, and look at us—we are the greatest!"

Because we live in the secular world, it is easy for this same spirit to infect the church. We get the same thrill of accomplishment. It goes, "Hey, look at my Sunday School pins!" or, "Did you notice our church attendance?" or, "Our church is in the top 10 percent in giving to the denomination." Christians often weary of this secular approach to rewards in the church because true celebration is more inclusive. When we celebrate in Christ, we are celebrating our unity in the family of faith. We are a part of God's kingdom where the spirit should be, "Hey, look at what happens when we join hands with God and each other to work together!"

Christians are not individual superstars who learn to play well together for the common good and greater reward. We are God's children who join together in the realization that in spite of our unloveliness, sin, and brokenness, God is redeeming us. We accept ourselves and each other because of the goodness and grace of God. That good news demands responses of gratitude to the Father and singing with surprise and joy when our accomplishments exceed our dreams. When we fail in our dreams, we know we are still loved and accepted by God, others, and ourselves. Faith is the support system which calls forth celebration whether we win or lose. Try that in the locker room when you have lost the superbowl!

Meaningful celebration is needed in both the small-task groups which do the work of ministry and the larger congregation of which they are a part. The forms of celebration in small groups and the larger group must be different. When we celebrate in one without including the other, the organic character of the church is not strengthened.

Small-group celebrations often lead to good large-group celebrations. Unfortunately, many small groups complete their work and fade out of existence without thanking either the Lord or allowing the congregation to affirm their work. It is important for those who have worked to become a good group, completed their tasks, and grown together to experience positive closure.

Positive closure begins with a good evaluation of the group's work. An official review of the mission statement and reminder of the boundaries and constraints affecting the group will help. Write the evaluation of each step followed on newsprint. (By now you should be aware that large amounts of newsprint will be consumed by good groups). Allow the sharing of humorous and sad stories of the journey in the group. Ask probing questions of accomplishment and discuss them such as:

- What have we learned about ourselves in this experience?
- How has our faith been strengthened? Challenged?
- What have we learned about each other?
- Are there improvements needed in the way our church functions?
- What were our disappointments in doing this work?

These, and other questions, can become the catalysts for personal affirmations. Out of the circle of conversation can come expressions of grace, "Tom, you taught me to trust the group to do its best. Thank you." "I have had a positive experience on a church committee for the first time in five years. This was a great moment for me." "I understand for the first time what it means to really pray for my church. We had so many problems in this ministry that the only way we got through was to depend on God."

Real fellowship is associated with eating and drinking in most church groups. Now is the time to break out the ice cream, coffee, soft drinks, cookies, or whatever the group likes for sharing the fun and good cheer. As the meeting concludes, ask the leader to close with words of appreciation to the group, join hands, and let the group share in prayer. Celebration is finally offering all we are and all we have done to the Father in thanksgiving.

Within a few days, the group leader should write each member a personal note of appreciation acknowledging the contribution of each and the group as a whole. Then communicate through avenues of churchwide information the work of the group with "well done" expressed as enthusiastically as possible.

This linkage with the larger church is crucial. We must help every church member understand the importance of individual and small-group contributions in the total life of the church. An example is the camping program of the Crescent Hill Baptist Church in Louisville, Kentucky. For years, the youth have traveled from Kentucky to North Carolina for two weeks of church camp. Each year when camp is closed and buses are loaded, hugs and tears push back the pain and grief of separation and change. When the youth and their leaders come down from the mountain, evaluation begins. Before it is completed, the teenagers are responsible for the next worship service at the church. Songs are sung, and sermons are shared as the teenagers tell their encounter with self, friends, and God. The celebration is contagious. It begins in a small planning group and moves through the entire congregation. The home folks are included. It is their camp, too! There is no better way to tell the story of Christian education through camping than with sixty or seventy celebrating teenagers in a worship service. Celebration communicates the good news. Do we dare not celebrate?

The need to celebrate is deep within us. Celebrations are opportunities for developing and expressing the Christian spirit, sharing information, interpreting ministry, and concouraging change. As we celebrate we learn to believe. We need to come to the party of Christian celebration.

Many of us have been taught: "If it's too much fun, it's not Christian." Celebration is more than fun, but it is that. Every Christian has reason to celebrate joyous faith. Even the painful times in a church's life can call forth joy. In the play *Zorba the Greek,* Zorba is an abysmal failure in all areas of his life. Yet he celebrates his failure as the best failure ever. He is able to dance and sing in freedom in spite of all that has gone wrong with him. A church in South Carolina discovered the Zorba spirit in celebration:

> The church was in conflict with the local association and the fellowship between churches was affected. Trust was destroyed when the association voted to withdraw fellowship from the church. A relationship that had lasted for generations was broken by that action. The people from the church huddled together in silence after the meeting and waited until the room cleared. Someone said, "Well, it's over. Let's go home." Another responded, "No, let's go to the church!" They drove forty miles to the church building in a sad caravan. They felt rejected, misunderstood, angry, hurt, and confused. A group of Christians with whom they felt common cause had told them they were no longer welcome.
>
> When the cars came to church, the members silently filed into the dark fellowship hall while someone reached for the lights. They sat down and talked about the event and their feelings. Then someone said, "Let's sing." And sing they did as spontaneously they moved from hymn to hymn. As they sang the songs of faith, the moods mellowed and changed. They prayed about the future.
>
> Someone slipped out to an all-night grocery, bought bacon and eggs, and returned to begin cooking. Soon smells of frying bacon filled the room. Some laughter could be heard. They ate and told stories about the life of the church through the years. The minister stood and called the group to its conviction and memory of faith. Taking bread from the meal, he made it a symbol of love, and in the hurt and pain of the evening a group of believers acknowledged their faith and commitment to God and each other.

We beseech you to make the power of celebration a part of the vitality of life in your church. Don't wait for a quarterly Lord's Supper service to reflect on the meaning of celebration in worship. Make the spirit of joy in Christ the heart of all organizational life.

Let the invitation be for
all who labor in the Kingdom.
Come! Come to the party of work in God's vineyard.
Amen.

Appendix 1
Models of Church Structures

A variety of choices exist in designing a church structure. The following options are made available as stimuli for those attempting to organize new structures or change old ones. These are intended to be suggestive of several possibilities.

One person

Having one person responsible for the tasks of ministry in a certain area is the easiest and simplest church structure. That person agrees to enlist as many others as needed to accomplish a task. He or she understands what needs to be done, how to do it, and will do it.

Small churches do their work best by securing a commitment from one person to be responsible for a program area. If the task can be done by one person, ask only one to do it. In multistaff congregations, a single staff person needs to be accountable for enlisting needed resources to fulfill a specific program.

Denominational Models

Some churches will choose to follow the recommended approach of the denomination. Every major denomination will have either a required or recommended pattern for the local congregation. Often the stable congregation in need of renewal has followed an older model which worked at the time it was implemented. But changes within the denomination, the community, or the congregation have not been monitored. Thus, a more effective organization could be developed. Resistance arises, however, because some feel to change the model is to betray the denomination.

Extensive literature is available from denominational agencies for organizing local churches. While it is not the intention of this book to review the patterns available, some guides for denominational families are included in the bibliography. You may wish to consult a variety of these sources to gain a more detailed understanding of how various denominations do their work. We will summarize the various approaches.

Advisory Organizations

Lay participation in some congregations is primarily advisory. All decisions are really made by the pastor, priest, or a powerful board. Even when possessing such authority, however, the wise leader will seek counsel from others concerning the decisions to be made and tasks to be performed. The advantages of this approach are that decisions can be made quickly, conflict is minimal, and everyone knows who is in charge. The disadvantages are lower levels of participation in the church, a lack of strong leaders, and lay withdrawal when there is disagreement with decisions. There are no avenues for democratic change, except as they

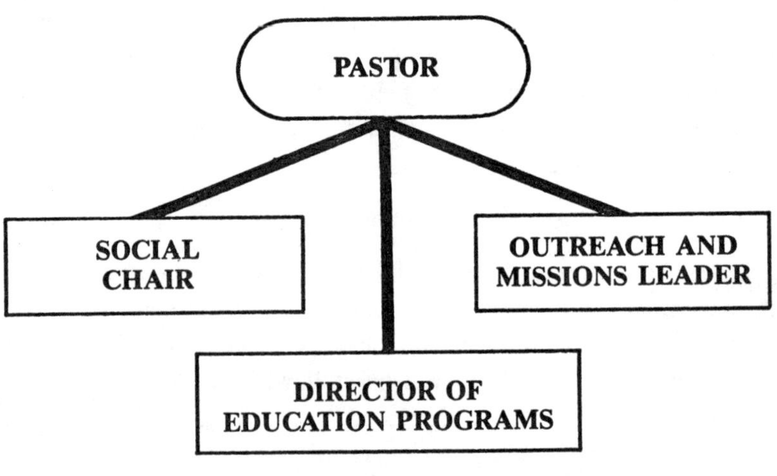

Organization for Small Churches

are allowed by the powerful leaders of the church.[1] In reality, many churches function this way, even though their formal documents and traditions emphasize another approach. The church in which all committees must have the agreement of a central body such as deacons or vestry members before approaching the congregation have an advisory organization.

Commission or Committee Structure

Some congregations invest most of the work of the church in an organization of committees or commissions. Each committee or commission is given a well-defined area of responsibility with written job require-

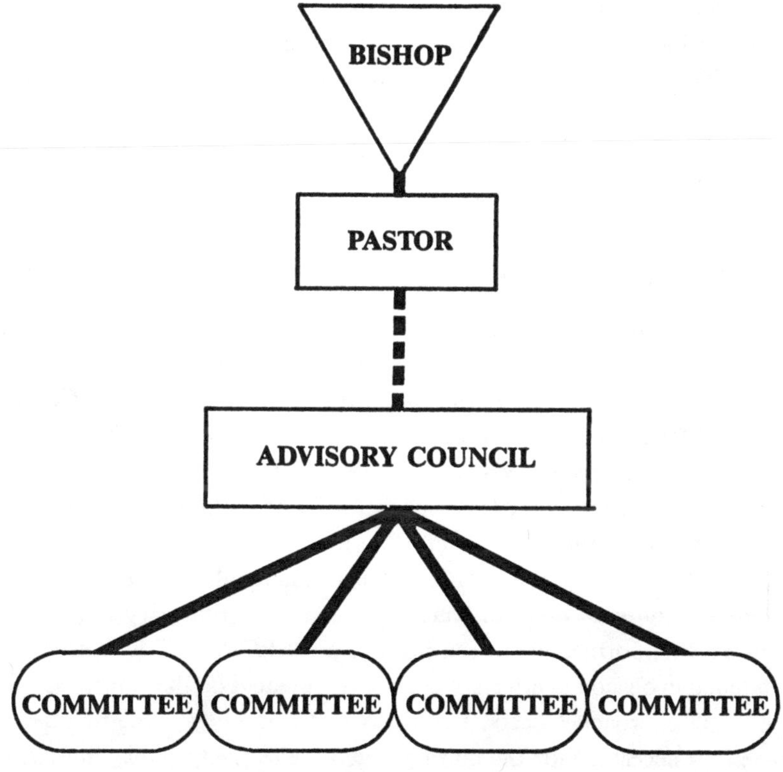

Advisory Model of Organization

ments. The congregation elects committee or commission members. In turn, these subgroups of the congregation are accountable only to the congregation for their work. Thus, they are delegated by the church to perform certain tasks in its behalf, and they report recommendations and activities directly to the church.

The advantages of this system are that the various tasks of the church can be identified clearly and assigned to one group. In this way, committees become staffed with church members who are specialists in those areas. The disadvantage is that such groups may function so expertly and independently that they do not communicate with each other. Because of this, confusion or duplication of effort often occur. An example of this is the finance committee which presents a budget to the church without consultation with other committees or the pastor. Strong committee or commission structures often lack coordination between them. It is also possible for such groups to become so specialized they fail to consider the needs of members not on their committee or represented on the committee.

Strong Church Council

Larger churches often combine the advantages of a strong committee structure with a strong Church Council to insure coordination between the committees. Thus, the tasks of creating and developing new ministries rests with committees who specialize in their area of work. Coordination is facilitated through regular council meetings of the chairpersons who coordinate recommendations, budget, staffing, calendar, and the flow of information to the larger church. The advantage of this approach is that responsibilities of committees are maintained while points of conflict between them are minimized. Councils also are helpful since there is representation from every group in the church. All groups in the church are informed about the respective work. Women, who are often excluded in deacon boards, are usually represented on the Church Council. Such approaches become complex and can increase the number of meetings necessary for the church to work effectively. Thus, the disadvantage is the problems of bureaucratic complexity.

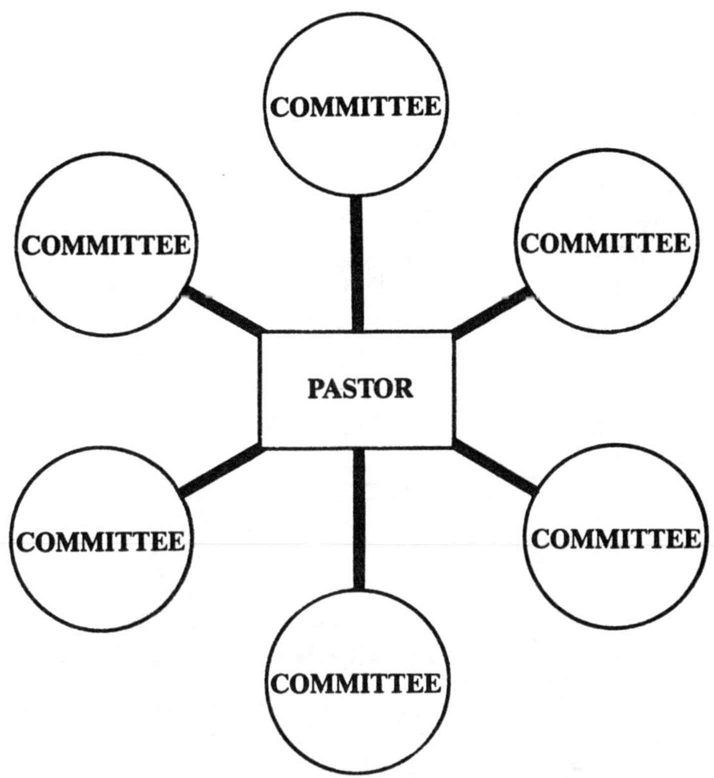

Committee Organizational Model

Central Power Group

Some churches organize themselves by delegating most congregational decisions and responsibilities to a small power group. This may be a board of deacons, elders, or vestry. Often such groups consist of older members only, exclude females from participation, and are not sensitive to the feelings of all of the groups in the congregation. This approach can be very efficient. Power groups tend to make decisions, implement them, and delegate tasks to others quickly and efficiently. The weaknesses are the lack of participation from newcomers, women, and youth, as well as low levels of ownership in the larger congregation and the loss of creativity.

Southern Baptist churches have no singular model of organization. The traditional model has been one of strong administrative authority residing in the body of deacons. This approach is still practiced in many older, small, and rural congregations. Since the mid-1960s, the denominational emphasis has been upon a strong Church Council approach with program organizations of Sunday School, Women's Missionary Union, Brotherhood, Music Program, Training Program, Program Services, and Administrative Services performing the tasks of ministry.[2] More recent emphases have maintained this strong council approach with a different arranging of program emphases than in former years. J.

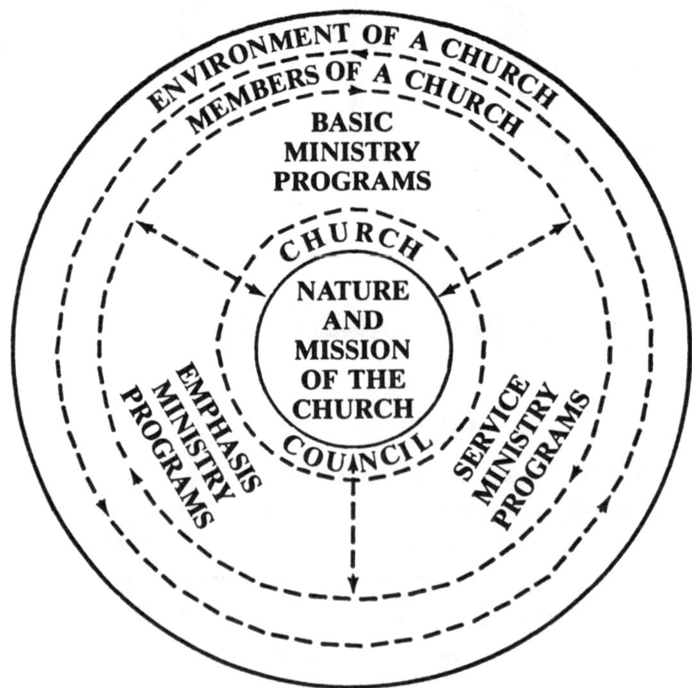

Church Council Organizational Model [3]

Ralph Hardee has proposed an excellent council structure organized around basic ministry programs, service ministry programs, and emphasis ministry programs. This accommodates newer programs of work added since the 1960s.[3]

Interchurch or Parachurch Structures

Some congregations have discovered that their goals of ministry beyond the church can sometimes be carried out more effectively by working with other churches. Most denominations have associational, district, synodical or presbyterial, or diocesan structures. They are usually designed to help congregations do their work more effectively or fulfill

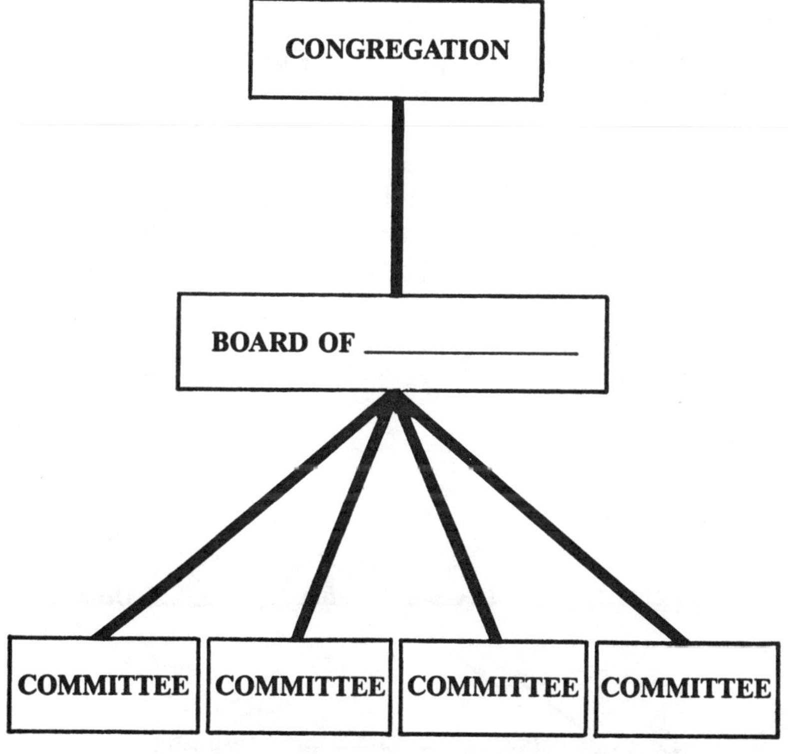

Central Board Administrative Structure

outcomes which individual congregations do not accomplish well alone. Beginning new churches, conducting community evangelistic campaigns, addressing a critical social issue, or meeting a large-scale community need like homelessness may call for interchurch structures.

One of the more common interchurch structures to emerge in recent years has been the neighborhood cluster ministry. A group of churches within the same community, often from different denominations, organizes a nonprofit corporation to conduct needed social ministries. Each participating church contributes money and board members. The board then sets policies and guides the direction of such a ministry.

Process model

Still another organizational model emphasizes process over structure. Most of the denominational approaches deal with the specific structures a church needs to accomplish its tasks. Thus, the mode of organization is task oriented.

The process approach attempts to identify the process inherent in the accomplishing of every task of ministry. Thus, the principle of leadership is to organize all work so that effective processes are insured. If the process is followed, the task will get done effectively. Thus, organizing is one step in the process of doing ministry.

One of the better processes for accomplishing ministry has been developed by Ernest O. White. He suggests there are seven essential tasks or

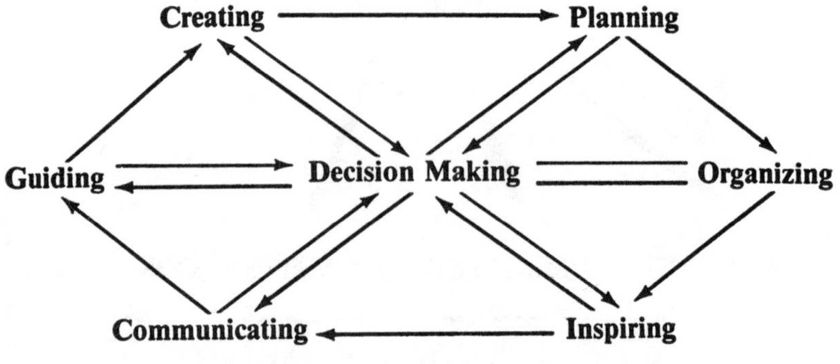

Process Model of Church Structure

processes inherent in all church leadership: creating, planning, organizing, inspiring, communicating, guiding, and decision making.[4] Thus, the process leader focuses upon how a group accomplishes each of these steps in the completion of the tasks of ministry in the church. Structure is a by-product of the planning process and fits every situation in terms of the uniqueness of that setting.

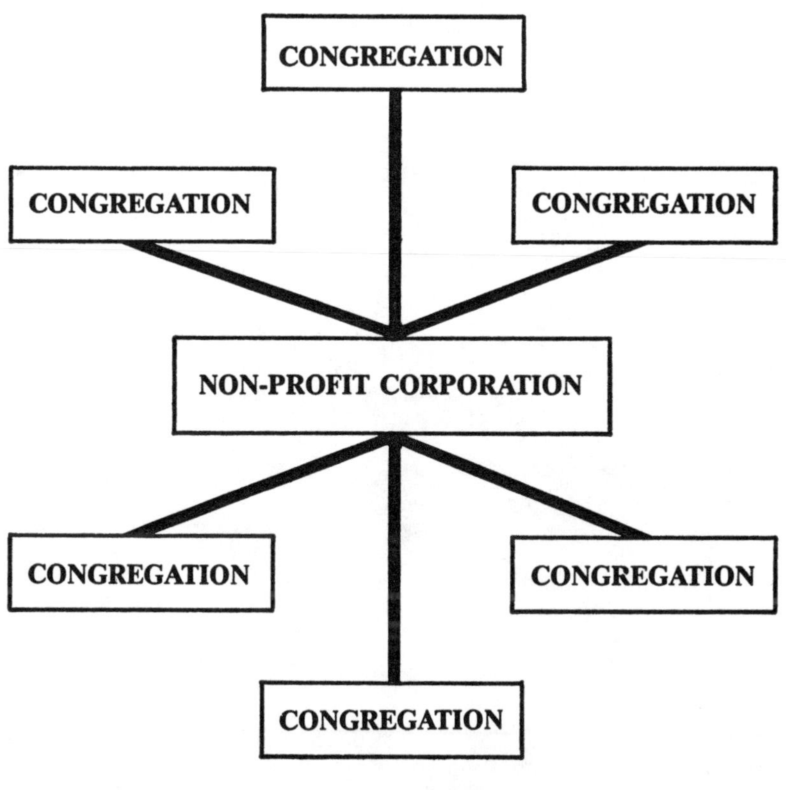

Cluster Ministry Organization

Appendix 2

A Practical Guide to Parliamentary Procedure

by Lee H. McCoy

A Practical Guide to Parliamentary Procedure

LEE H. McCOY

(For more complete information refer to Robert's Rules of Order Revised)

CLASSIFICATION OF MOTIONS	ORDER OF PRECEDENCE[1]	MOTIONS	INTERRUPT A SPEAKER?	A SECOND REQUIRED?	MAY BE DEBATED?	MAY BE AMENDED?	VOTE REQUIRED?	PURPOSE OF MOTION
I. PRIVILEGED MOTIONS The highest in rank and of such importance that they permit the main business of the body to be set aside.	1	To fix the time to adjourn	No	Yes	No	Yes[2]	Majority	To set a time (and place) for the next meeting
	2	To adjourn	No	Yes	No	No	Majority	To terminate the meeting (to the next regular meeting)
	3	To take a recess	No	Yes	No	Yes[2]	Majority	To secure an intermission in the proceedings
	4	To raise a question of privilege	Yes	No	No	No	None[3]	To protect the rights of the body or of an individual
	5	To call for the orders of the day	Yes	No	No	No	None[3]	To insist on conforming to the order of business
II. SUBSIDIARY MOTIONS Used to modify or help dispose of other motions. They can be offered only in the order of their rank and must be voted on before returning to the original motion.	6	To lay on the table	No	Yes	No	No	Majority	To postpone temporarily so as to attend to other matters
	7	To call for the previous question	No	Yes	No	No	Two-Thirds	To stop debate and bring the pending question to vote
	8	To limit or extend limits of debate	No	Yes	No	Yes	Two-Thirds	To decrease or increase the allowable time for discussion
	9	To postpone to a definite time	No	Yes	Yes	Yes	Majority	To delay action until a later time
	10	To refer to a committee	No	Yes	Yes	Yes	Majority	To place in hands of a small group for study
	11	To amend	No	Yes	Yes	Yes	Majority	To change the wording of a pending motion
	12	To postpone indefinitely	No	Yes	Yes	No	Majority	To prevent a vote on the main question
III. THE MAIN MOTION The lowest in rank. All other motions take precedence over it in the order of their rank.	13	To make a main motion	No	Yes	Yes	Yes	Majority	To bring a matter before the body for its consideration and action

CLASSIFICATION OF MOTIONS	ORDER OF PRECEDENCE[1]	MOTIONS	INTERRUPT A SPEAKER?	A SECOND REQUIRED?	MAY BE DEBATED?	MAY BE AMENDED?	VOTE REQUIRED?	PURPOSE OF MOTION
IV. INCIDENTAL MOTIONS These arise "incidentally" out of discussions of pending business. They take precedence and must be decided before voting on the question from which they arise. They are lower in rank than privileged motions and generally yield to the motion to lay on the table.	All incidental motions are of equal rank. None can be displaced by one of the others.	To raise a point of order	Yes	No	No	No	None[3]	To call attention to a violation of the rules
		To appeal from the decision of the Chair	Yes	Yes	Yes	No	Majority	To obtain opinion of the body on the ruling of the Chair
		To call for a division of the body	Yes	No	No	No	None[3]	To determine the accuracy of the voice vote
		To call for a division of a question	Yes[2]	Yes[2]	No	Yes	Majority	To discuss by parts for more careful consideration
		To object to the consideration of a matter	Yes	No	No	No	Two-Thirds	To prevent discussion of irrelevant questions
		To make a parliamentary inquiry	Yes	No	No	No	None[3]	To secure parliamentary information when in doubt
		To withdraw or modify a motion	Yes	No	No	No	None[3]	To allow person making motion to withdraw or change it
		To suspend the rules	No	Yes	No	No	Two-Thirds	To permit action prohibited by a particular rule
		To make nominations	No	No	Yes	No	Majority	To present names for consideration to fill offices
		To close nominations	No	Yes	No	Yes	Two-Thirds	To prevent other names from being placed in nomination
V. MISCELLANEOUS MOTIONS Have characteristics of their own. Do not fit into any of the other classifications.	See footnotes 6 and 7.	To take from the table	No	Yes	No	No	Majority	To consider business that temporarily has been set aside
		To reconsider a question	Yes	Yes	Yes[8]	No	Majority	To reopen for discussion and decision a matter previously considered and voted upon

1. When any one of the motions is immediately pending, those above it are in order and those below it are out of order (IV and V excepted).
2. Restricted. See **Robert's Rules of Order Revised.**
3. The Chair decides. If appealed, then majority decides.
4. An amendment to an amendment cannot be amended.
5. Only one main motion can be considered at a time.
6. Takes precedence over no pending question. It is in order only during that meeting or the next. It is proposed under "new business." It yields to privileged and incidental motion, but not to subsidiary.
7. Can be made only by one voting with the prevailing side. While having high precedence as to "entry," it has precedence only over other main motion and to take from the table.
8. Undebatable only when the motion to be reconsidered is undebatable.

This is a reprint from the August 1964 issue of Church Administration.

Notes

Chapter 1

1. Philip B. Gove, ed., *Webster's Third New International Dictionary* (Springfield, Mass.: World Publishing Co., 1965), p. 1590.

2. Ibid.

3. Gaines S. Dobbins, *A Ministering Church.* (Nashville: Broadman Press, 1960), p. 32.

4. Each of these functions can be explored more fully by examining the biblical meaning for each in the *Theological Dictionary of the New Testament,* Vol. I-VII, ed. by Gerhard Kittel, trans. by Geoffrey W. Bromily (Grand Rapids: Wm. B. Eerdmans Publishing Co., 1964).

5. Dobbins, *A Ministering Church,* pp. 32.

Chapter 2

1. Rudee D. Boan, "Southern Baptist Church-Type Missions: Origin, Development, and Outcome, 1979-1984." Unpublished Ph.D. dissertation, The Southern Baptist Theological Seminary, Louisville, Ky., Dec. 1985.

2. Robert D. Dale, *To Dream Again* (Nashville: Broadman Press, 1981).

3. Quoted in Reginald M. McDonough, "Roads that Lead to Somewhere," *The Baptist Program,* June/July 1985, p. 35.

4. Kennon L. Callahan, *Twelve Keys to an Effective Church* (San Francisco: Harper and Row Publishers, 1983), pp. 1-9.

5. David A. Roozen, William McKinney, and Jackson W. Carroll, *Varieties of Religious Presence: Mission in Public Life* (New York: The Pilgrim Press, 1984), pp. 100-144.

6. Ibid., pp. 177-216.

7. Ibid., pp. 145-176.

8. Ibid., pp. 217-246.

9. Ronald G. Capelle, *Changing Human Systems* (Toronto, Canada: International Human Systems Institute, 1979), p. 2.

10. Lyle E. Schaller, *Effective Church Planning* (Nashville: Abingdon Press, 1979), pp. 17-63 explores the multiple differences between small groups and large groups and how one relates differently depending on the size of the group. See also Lyle E. Schaller, *Looking in the Mirror: Self-Appraisal in the Local Church* (Nashville: Abingdon Press, 1984), pp.

14-37; and Arlin J. Rothauge, *Sizing Up a Congregation for New Member Ministry*, (New York: Episcopal Church Center, n.d.).

Chapter 3

1. Robert D. Dale, *Ministers as Leaders* (Nashville: Broadman Press, 1984).
2. Ibid., pp. 18-25.
3. Kennon L. Callahan, *Twelve Keys to an Effective Church* (San Francisco: Harper and Row Publishers, 1983), pp. 59-60.
4. Douglas W. Johnson, *The Care and Feeding of Volunteers*, Creative Leadership Series, ed. Lyle E. Schaller (Nashville: Abingdon Press, 1978) has many other helpful suggestions for recruiting and working with volunteers.
5. Lyle E. Schaller, *Survival Tactics in the Parish* (Nashville: Abingdon Press, 1977), pp. 80-90.

Chapter 4

1. Daniel Yankelovich, *New Rules: Searching for Self-Fulfillment in a World Turned Upside Down* (New York: Random House, 1981), p. xiv.

Chapter 5

1. Larry L. McSwain and William C. Treadwell, Jr., *Conflict Ministry in the Church* (Nashville: Broadman Press, 1981); Speed B. Leas, *Leadership and Conflict*, Creative Leadership Series, ed. Lyle E. Schaller (Nashville: Abingdon Press, 1982); and Speed B. Leas, *Moving Your Church Through Conflict* (Washington, D.C.: Alban Institute, 1985).
2. Leas, *Moving Your Church Through Conflict*, pp. 19-22.
3. McSwain and Treadwell, *Conflict Ministry in the Church*, pp. 41-45; Leas, *Moving Your Church Through Conflict*, pp. 29-33.
4. Speed B. Leas, *Discover Your Conflict Management Style* (Washington, D.C.: Alban Institute, 1984), pp. 8-23.
5. Ibid.

Chapter 6

1. John Naisbitt, *Reinventing the Corporation* (New York: Warner Books, 1985).
2. Ibid., p. 20.
3. Ibid., p. 24.
4. Robert D. Dale, *To Dream Again* (Nashville: Broadman Press, 1981).
5. Ibid., pp. 105-126.
6. Kennon L. Callahan, *Twelve Keys to an Effective Church* (San Francisco: Harper and Row Publications, 1983), pp. 35-39.
7. See Carl S. Dudley, *Where Have All Our People Gone? New Choices for Old Churches* (New York: The Pilgrim Press, 1979); and Robert T. Gibbons, *Half the Congregation: Ministry with 18 to 40 Year Olds* (Washington, D.C.: Alban Institute, 1984).
8. See Edgar H. Schein, "The Mechanisms of Change," and Kenneth D. Benne and Max Birnbaum, "Principles of Changing" in *The Planning of Change* ed. Warren G.

Bennis, Kenneth D. Benne, and Robert Chin (New York: Holt, Rinehart and Winston, Inc., 1969), pp. 98-107, 328-335.

Appendix 1

1. George M. Williams, *Improving Parish Management: Working Smarter, Not Harder* (Mystic, Conn.: Twenty-Third Publications, 1983), pp. 76-78 advises freedom to make decisions by advisory councils.

2. W. L. Howse and W. O. Thomason, *A Church Organized and Functioning* (Nashville: Convention Press, 1963) provided the standard organizational model for SBC churches during the past two decades.

3. J. Ralph Hardee, "Church Organization," *Church Administration Handbook* ed. Bruce P. Powers (Nashville: Broadman Press, 1985), pp. 32-65 is a comprehensive guide to church committee functions with a strong council structure.

4. Ernest O. White, *Becoming a Christian Leader* (Nashville: Convention Press, 1985), p. 42.

Bibliography

American Management Association. *How to Improve Managerial Performance.* N.P.: AMACOM, 1958.

Benne, Kenneth D. and Max Birnbaum, "Principles of Changing," *The Planning of Change* ed. by Warren G. Bennis, Kenneth D. Benne and Robert Chin. New York: Holt, Rinehart and Winston, Inc., 1969, pp. 328-335.

Boan, Rudee D. "Southern Baptist Church-Type Missions: Origin, Development, and Outcome, 1979-1984." Unpublished Ph.D. dissertation, The Southern Baptist Theological Seminary, American Management Association, *How to Improve Managerial Performance.* N.P.: AMACOM, 1958.

Benne, Kenneth D., and Birnbaum, Max. "Principles of Changing," *The Planning of Change.* Edited by Warren G. Bennis, Kenneth D. Benne, and Robert Chin. New York: Holt, Rinehart and Winston, Inc., 1969.

Boan, Rudee D. "Southern Baptist Church-Type Missions: Origin, Development, and Outcome, 1979-1984." Unpublished Ph.D. dissertation, The Southern Baptist Theological Seminary. Louisville, Ky., December 1985.

Callahan, Kennon L. *Twelve Keys to an Effective Church.* San Francisco: Harper and Row Publishers, 1983.

Capelle, Ronald G. *Changing Human Systems.* Toronto: International Human Systems Institute, 1979.

Carroll, Jackson W.; Dudley, Carl S.; and McKinney, William. *Handbook for Congregational Studies.* Nashville: Abingdon Press, 1986.

Clapp, Steve. *Positioning Ministry for Success.* Champaign, Il.: C-4 RESOURCES, 1984.

Dale, Robert D. *To Dream Again: How to Help Your Church Come Alive.* Nashville: Broadman Press, 1981.

———. *Ministers As Leaders.* Nashville: Broadman Press, 1984.

Dobbins, Gaines S. *A Ministering Church.* Nashville: Broadman Press, 1961.

Dudley, Carl S., ed. *Building Effective Ministry: Theory and Practice in the Local Church.* San Francisco: Harper & Row, 1983.

———. *Where Have All Our People Gone? New Choices for Old Churches.* New York: The Pilgrim Press, 1979.

Gribbons, Robert T. *Half the Congregation: Ministry with 18 to 40 Year Olds.* Washington, D.C.: Alban Institute, 1984.

Graves, Harold K. *The Nature and Functions of a Church.* Nashville: Broadman Press, 1963.

Gove, Philip B. ed., *Webster's Third New International Dictionary.* Springfield, Mass.: G. and C. Merriam Co., 1965.

Hardee, J. Ralph. "Church Organization," *Church Administration Handbook.* Edited by Bruce P. Powers. Nashville: Broadman Press, 1985.

Hersey, Paul, and Blanchard, Kenneth H. *Management of Organizational Behavior: Utilizing Human Resources,* 3rd ed. Englewood Cliffs, N.J.: Prentice-Hall, Inc. 1977 [1969].

Howse, W. L., and Thomason, W. O. *A Church Organized and Functioning.* Nashville: Broadman Press, 1963.

Johnson, Douglas W. *The Care and Feeding of Volunteers.* Creative Leadership Series. Edited by Lyle E. Schaller. Nashville: Abingdon Press, 1978.

Kittel, Gerhard, ed. *Theological Dictionary of the New Testament,* Vol. I-VIII. Translated by Geoffrey W. Bromiley. Grand Rapids: Eerdmans Publishing Co., 1964—.

Leas, Speed B. *Discover Your Conflict Management Style.* Washington, D.C.: Alban Institute, 1984.

———. *Leadership and Conflict.* Creative Leadership Series ed. by Lyle E. Schaller. Nashville: Abindgon Press, 1982.

———. *Moving Your Church Through Conflict.* Washington, D.C.: Alban Institute, 1985.

McDonough, Reginald M. "Roads that Lead to Somewhere." In *The Baptist Program,* June/July 1985, p. 35.

McSwain, Larry L.; and Treadwell, William C., Jr. *Conflict Ministry in the Church.* Nashville: Broadman Press, 1981.

Naisbitt, John. *Reinventing the Corporation.* New York: Warner Books, 1985.

Pendorf, James G.; and Lundquist, Helmer C. *Church Organization: A Manual for Effective Local Church Administration.* Wilton, Conn.: Morehouse-Barlow, 1977.

Powers, Bruce P., ed. *Church Administration Handbook.* Nashville: Broadman Press, 1985.

Roozen, David A.; McKinney, William; and Carroll, Jackson W. *Varieties of Religious Experience: Mission in Public Life.* New York: The Pilgrim Press, 1984.

Rothauge, Arlin J. *Sizing Up a Congregation for New Member Ministry.* New York: Episcopal Church Center, n.d.

Saarinen, Martin F. *The Life Cycle of a Congregation.* Washington, D.C.: The Alban Institute, 1985.

Schaller, Lyle E. *Effective Church Planning.* Nashville: Abingdon Press, 1979.

———. *The Multiple Staff and the Larger Church.* Nashville: Abingdon Press, 1980.

———. *Activating the Passive Church: Diagnosis and Treatment.* Nashville: Abingdon Press, 1983.

———. *The Small Church is Different!* Nashville: Abingdon Press, 1982.

Schein, Edgar H., "The Mechanisms of Change," *The Planning of Change.* Edited by Warren G. Bennis, Kenneth D. Benne, and Robert Chin. New York: Holt, Rinehart and Winston, Inc., 1969.

Short, Mark. "Administration in a Small Church," *Church Administration Handbook.* Edited by Bruce P. Powers. Nashville: Broadman Press, 1985.

Walrath, Douglas Alan. *Leading Churches Through Change.* Creative

Leadership Series. Edited by Lyle E. Schaller. Nashville: Abingdon Press, 1979.

White, Ernest O. *Becoming a Christian Leader.* Nashville: Convention Press, 1985.

Williams, George. *Improving Parish Management.* Mystic, Conn.: Twenty-Third Publications, 1983.

Yankelovich, Daniel. *New Rules: Searching for Self-Fulfillment in a World Turned Upside Down.* New York: Random House, 1981.